My Platinum Years

By Ginny Nickoloff

DANCING CROWS
PRESS

Copyright 2021© Virginia Nickoloff: All rights reserved. No part of this book may be used or reproduced in any manner whatsoever without written permission except in the case of brief quotations embodied in critical articles and reviews.

ISBN: 978-1-951543-12-9

Cover art by Colin Wheeler, MFA, ABD
strickenbrow@gmail.com

DancingCrowsPress@gmail.com

Printed in the United States of America

Dedication

For my Sons, Grandchildren and Great-grandchildren and especially my Daughter-in-Law, Jessica, who puts up with my idiosyncrasies. May you all enjoy your Platinum Years with Gusto, as I have.

Acknowledgments

Special thanks to Elyse Wheeler, my editor, extraordinaire, and her son, Colin for his cover design.

Chapter	Contents	Page
One	Planning: Visiting All the States	1
Two	Planning: Around the World in 48 Days: England	28
Three	Egypt	36
Four	India	52
Five	Bali	64
Six	Korea	72
Seven	Australia	75
Eight	Anglesea	87
Nine	Vietnam and Cambodia	98
Ten	Cuba and Family Reunions	123
Eleven	Exercise and Diet	129
Twelve	Pets and Plants	132
Thirteen	Jessie and Tony	141
Fourteen	Poetry	145
Fifteen	Letters	174
Sixteen	Opera	203
Seventeen	Jokes	210
Eighteen	Lists	218
Nineteen	Politics	232
Twenty	Extra-Curricular	237
Twenty-One	Books	247
Twenty-Two	Words	254
Twenty-Three	Genealogy	257
Twenty-Four	Photography	261
Twenty-Five	Memories	282
Twenty-Six	Prayer	291

Chapter One
Planning: Visiting All the States

I choose to think of the Golden Years as the time between ages 55 to 75 which brings me to the Platinum Years, ages 75 to 95 … and beyond! Since I am 96, four years older than Mickey Mouse, I choose to think my grey hair has become platinum blonde, and every new day is a jewel to be treasured. For all the Golden and Platinum Year-Olds who might want to read this, it will be printed in large type!

To what do I attribute my Platinum Years? Sometime in my thirties, I read an article about a man who never caught colds or flu. Whenever he sneezed, he stood on his head for one minute. After 9 or 10 years old, standing on my head wasn't an option for me so I came up with the idea that, while standing, I put my head down and raise my arms above my head and count fast to 125. This wasn't always feasible, so I came up with a few alternatives. If I was in a market when I sneezed, I pretended I was looking for something on the bottom shelf. If driving when I sneezed or riding on an elephant, I held my breath until my face got red. The neighborhood kids thought I was weird, and my kids explained my odd behavior: "Oh, she just sneezed!"

I theorized forcing the blood to my head brought white corpuscles to fight any infection I might have picked up. For whatever reason, the result of this crazy action has protected me all these years from catching flu or colds. And, more up to date, from catching corona virus so far in 2020.

Also, for some strange reason, I can honestly say I have never had a headache. A few years ago, I hosted a bridge party and one of the girls asked me if I had some aspirin. When I brought her the bottle, she said, "Ginny, these aspirin expired in 1985!"

This paragraph is reserved for women over forty. One day I was conversing with my gynecologist, Dr. James I. Wargin, who delivered all my babies. It was probably in the 1950's, and he told me some doctors had gone to a town in Mexico to see why the women there never had sweating problems when they were going through the change of life. The doctors figured out it was because of their diet of sweet potatoes. The doctors came back to this country and started a company called

Syntex making hormones out of sweet potatoes. It soon became number one on the Stock Exchange. I immediately started eating sweet potatoes or yams and breezed through menopause with no sweats! So, my advice: just eat sweet potatoes and I still do, as they are probably good for a lot of other things.

One other suggestion, if you have leg cramps, drink a glass of water with a teaspoonful of apple cider vinegar in the water. I suggested this to a friend and she mistakenly started to drink a glass of apple cider vinegar instead of putting a spoonful in the water. She almost choked to death … so be careful. Put it in water!

I think I owe my good teeth to the fact I hated Coca Cola. Early in my years, I discovered I didn't like Coke. Really, I didn't like carbonation. Then I read drinking Coke was like passing a tablespoon of sugar over your teeth. This didn't seem like a good idea, so I stuck to black coffee and tea with lemon. I avoided beer because it is fattening but I do enjoy wine and dry martinis on the rocks, not in a stem glass.

One thing to remember when you sit down to eat, (hopefully you don't eat on the run) your stomach is the size of your two fists put together, so don't eat more than that amount! It is also very nice if you can eat at a regular time every day. I eat at eight a.m., 12 noon, and 6 p.m. if possible.

When my Dad was in his eighties, he told me the best thing that can happen at his age is a good bowel movement every day. Well, I'm not saying it is the best thing, but it sure is a good thing!

One of the best things, though, is Wine Time at 5 p.m. with a few chips and dip. I am a very lucky gal who has three sons who call me on the phone in rotation at 5 p.m. to share wine time with me. Now during the corona epidemic, we call it "quarantini time." Jim calls from Miami Beach, Jac calls from Colorado and Tom calls from Kennesaw, Georgia. Tom usually visits me on Sunday, and we watch a Braves game or Falcon football or an old movie together.

Enough of my longevity. In my Golden Years, I was blessed with a fun-loving husband who retired from his law practice at fifty-five when his secretary said, "Jim, you are fired, and I quit!"

Soon, we sold our house in Sierra Madre and moved to the desert to escape the smog engulfing the Los Angeles basin. Apple Valley had an airport and Jimmy who already had a plane was happy. When we flew in the Los Angeles area and landed through the smog, the smell was horrible.

We had ten enjoyable years in the clean air of Apple Valley. Jimmy and I flew his twin-engine Seneca to Arizona, New Mexico, and to the ski slopes at Mammoth and Lake Tahoe. I was the navigator, usually following highways down below and watching out for other planes. I even took flying lessons but never had the guts to solo. Jimmy also had an acrobatic plane I also never had the guts to fly, with him doing loop the loops.

Then Jimmy became obsessed with wanting to build a Glasair TD. TD means tail dragger. One day, a big flatbed truck drove up in front of our house in Apple Valley loaded with airplane parts. Jimmy knew nothing about building an airplane, but, fortunately, some of his friends had worked at Lockheed and gave him their help. He started the building in our three-car garage. Our cars were relegated to the wind and weather.

About this time, I was bent on remodeling our house which involved removing parts of it. One day, I said to Jimmy, "You are going to have to move that wing out of that room because the room won't be here after today." That was the first time he realized what I was doing! My son, Jon, and his friend, Mike, built a low brick wall on the edge of the road of our circular driveway. That took so long we dubbed it the "Chinese Wall." At the point where you entered and departed the driveway, Jon built five-foot-tall brick lamp posts.

When the big day arrived, and Jimmy was going to take the airplane body out to the airport to attach the wings, I could see the tail was going to hit the lamppost. He was a little hard of hearing and didn't hear me yelling to stop as he knocked down the post. I was unhappy, but he was ecstatic because it didn't damage the tail at all!

It took eight years of sanding fiber glass, gluing parts together and installing the engine. On my birthday, he said, "I think I will fly the little bird for the first time today." My heart sank and he promised to wait until the next day. I came home from playing golf and he was grinning from ear to ear. "You flew it didn't

you?" He said he was just going to test it on the runway and it just took off and the next thing he knew, he was flying!

We had thought about buying a condo while in Georgia at a stockholder's meeting for Mexican Specialties, Inc., a restaurant chain headquartered in Atlanta and founded by our No. 3 son, Tom. Our friends, Perk and Dee, also stockholders, suggested we spend the week with them at a time-share they had near Atlanta. Arriving at the airport in the pitch dark about 10 p.m., I asked Dee, "Why are we going west when Atlanta is north of the airport?"

Awaking the next morning, I looked out the window of the condo, and there was a beautiful lake! Coming from one of the driest states in the Union, I could not believe my eyes! All that water! We four had breakfast at the country club, and each couple found a real estate agent.

Jimmy and I were waiting in the back yard of a house on the lake for our real estate agent to get the key. Jimmy looked in the basement windows and said: "I could build a pontoon airplane in here and land it on the lake!" I said, "What makes you think they would let you land on the lake?" But I hoped I would like the house as I knew this was the house we were going to buy! We just up and moved from California to Georgia … and so did Perk and Dee!

It was love at first sight. Fairfield Plantation, a gated community, has an 18-hole golf course and a beautiful lake. Our five sons had left the nest and we were free to play golf and travel. Jimmy was happy West Georgia airport was close by.

First things first for him was getting his two planes to Georgia. He called me from California and said he and a friend were going to fly the two planes tandem leaving at dawn. The day went on and I heard nothing. I called to see if they had left, and no one knew anything. Finally, at 10 p.m. that night, I was frantic when I got a phone call from Mississippi. They had eaten a nice dinner and were going to bed. Expect them about noon the next day.

I got lost trying to find the airport and finally saw some people there. I asked if they had seen anyone landing and they said a Seneca had landed and pointed to Jimmy coming down the runway with the cockpit cover off and his hair flying. I can't describe my relief!

Now, he thought he was in heaven enjoying all the local pilots, but also realizing Georgia is full of trees and no big open landing places like the California desert offered. Then a pacemaker meant he couldn't fly without a licensed pilot with him. He sold the Seneca.

We walked early every morning, holding hands and life was beautiful until one day, Jimmy played golf, worked on a house project and needed something at the hardware store. On the way home, he got a ticket speeding on Highway 166. He decided there was nothing worth watching on TV that evening, so he chopped some wood and built a fire so we could read and enjoy the crackling. He left this world in the middle of that night, one month before the new millennium. He and I were 75 years old. I sold the Glassair to a pilot from Texas who had also built a plane. Thankfully, because Jimmy retired at 55, he lived all his Golden Years to the maximum.

A few years later, I was attending a Super Bowl party at a friend's house. Sitting next to me was a golfing friend of my husband who had lost his wife. We made the incredible discovery that his family had lived in Sierra Madre, California, a tiny town two miles long and one mile wide in the 1950's and where Jimmy and I had lived from 1950 to 1981. And so, my Platinum Years began linked to my boyfriend, Bob Fischer. Early on I told Bob that his 53 married years and my 52 married years were quite enough. We never lived together, but we traveled the world together.

The first time Bob asked me to play golf with him, I was startled to see on the passenger side of his golf cart, a metal plate: "California Native." His wife was born in San Diego. My birthplace, Santa Ana! How weird is that? Bob and I played in the Friday night Hit and Giggle Tournaments. I made my first hole-in-one playing with Jimmy in the Hit and Giggle on hole 16, and my second one three days before my 77th birthday on hole 8. (I just had to brag a little!)

The great thing about golf is it is a sport that can be played well into the Platinum Years. Our club's annual Dixie Open has been held every September for the last 40 years. I played in the Dixie Open when I was 90. There was a separate pitching contest where the player pitched over a sand trap and onto the putting green to hole Number 16. The closest to the hole would win the prize, a Nike golf bag. In the tournament I started on hole 18 so I was the first person to try this contest by the clubhouse. I pitched to 6 inches from the designated hole. Thinking that there were 100 girls playing behind me, it never occurred to me that I would be the closest. Giving out the prizes after the luncheon, the Pro called my name to win the golf bag. He said he had tried sixteen times and never got as close as I did and "she is 90!"

Bob and I also joined the Grasshoppers, a golfing group who played golf on weekends in the Carolinas and all over Georgia. Golf in the daytime and Mexican Train at night in hotel lobbies wherever we were playing.

We (Bob and I will become "we") compared notes and discovered he had been in every state but Maine, North Dakota. Idaho, and Alaska. I was missing Maine, Iowa, North Dakota and Alaska. So, obviously, our first driving trip was Georgia to Maine and down the Mississippi River to Iowa. Maine and Iowa: Mission accomplished, but I was still missing North Dakota and Alaska. Bob still needed those two also plus Idaho.

We planned to continue down the Mississippi River to New Orleans ... but it was not to be. While driving south, our highway was suddenly rumbling with army vehicles heading south. Hurricane Katrina was wreaking havoc and we were forced to turn east and stay in a little town that had signs in the windows ... no credit cards accepted because the credit card headquarters are in New Orleans and the city was completely shut down. Luckily, we had enough cash for dinner and a hotel room that night and then we headed home to Georgia.

Travelers at heart, we joined the Fairfield Plantation Travel Club and much to our delight, the first trip the group planned was sailing to Alaska. The year was 2002. On the ship one night, having imbibed in a few martinis, we attempted to dance to "Mama's on the Chain Gang" on a raised glass dance floor with colored lights flashing through. When we stepped down off the dance floor, a man announced: "That couple leaving the dance floor are the winners of the dance contest." We didn't even know we were in a contest. When he presented us with two coffee mugs with the ship's logo, I asked him, "Why did you pick us?" He said, "Because you were having the most fun."

Another "high-low" light of this trip was playing golf at Black Diamond Golf Club near Denali National Park (eaten up by humongous mosquitos). This satisfied our visit to Alaska, the 49th state.

In 2009, we figured out how we could complete our goal of seeing all 50 states: Anniston, Alabama to Idaho and back on Amtrak! This took a bit of planning with two goals in sight: North Dakota for Bob and me, and Idaho for Bob.

We loved having dinner at The Olive Tree restaurant or Gabe's in Villa Rica and hearing and watching the train go by at 7 pm. On this trip, we drove to the Anniston train station, just over the Georgia border in Alabama, to board the train (easier than driving to Atlanta and with no parking problem) and we waved to the Olive Tree and Gabe's Restaurants on the way by.

The first leg to Charlottesville, Virginia was uncomfortably spent in coach and we arrived 45 minutes late. The smiles on our faces didn't reflect what our bodies thought.

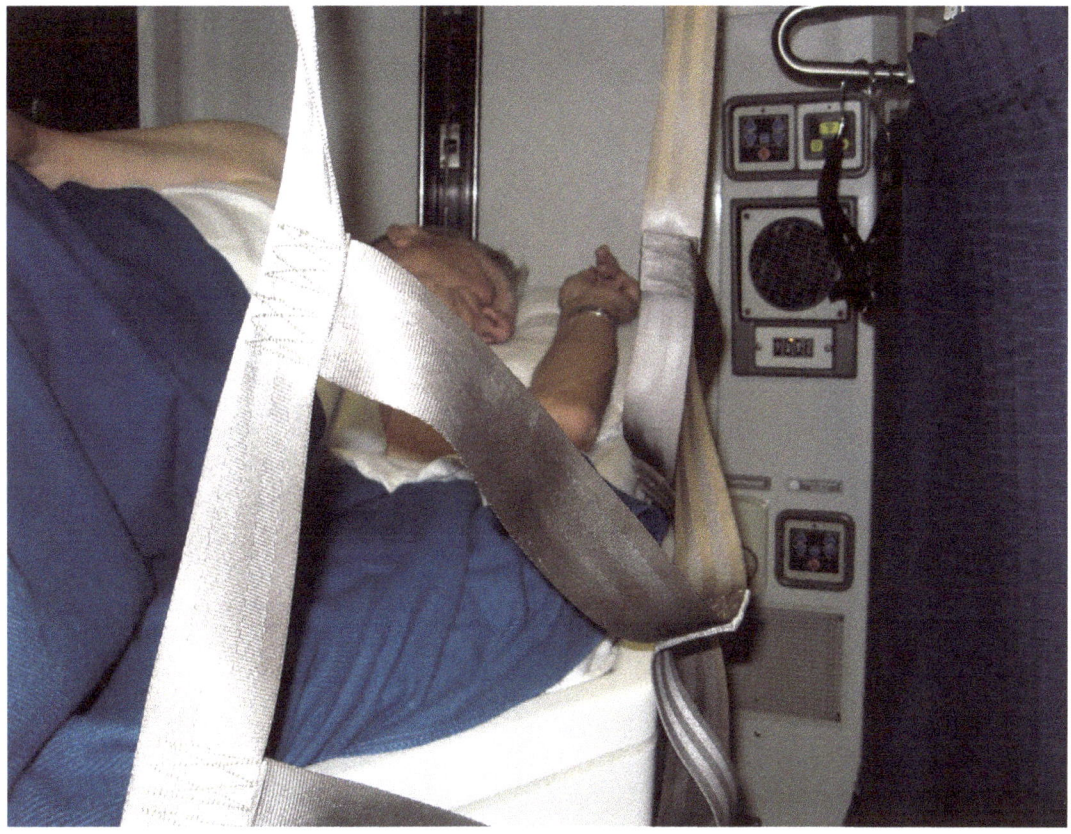

Arriving late didn't matter as we had a 6-hour layover before boarding the "Cardinal" for Chicago. Our "roomette" on the Cardinal was hardly more comfortable than the coach. Bob was warned to make sure his belt was fastened so he didn't fall out of the upper bunk.

When the bunks were in position, we had absolutely no room to stand in. Trying to get dressed in the morning was a Laurel and Hardy Comedy act. The shower was down the hall. Fortunately, the food was good on the train and we arrived in Chicago's huge Union Station and made an interesting discovery. People in the Midwest still ride the trains en masse. The station was really bustling, and we decided to take a little walk around Chicago … well, around the block.

Boarding the "Empire Builder," we were able to get coach seats on the upper deck with a great view of the Mississippi River as we passed Minneapolis and enjoyed a dinner of lamb shanks, corn, and mashed potatoes and Chardonnay topped off with a fabulous peanut butter cup cheesecake. Okay … how do I remember that? When I travel, I write in a journal every night describing the day's activities and I am teased by my son Jim that the journals are mostly about food.

We arrived at our first "destination," Rugby, North Dakota at 7 a.m. I had chosen Rugby, North Dakota, because it is the "center of the North American Continent." I had contacted a bed and breakfast on the internet and knew there were no taxis in this small town. They said to just call them when we arrived, and they would pick us up at the train station. The population is 2,876 making Rugby the eighteenth largest city in North Dakota.

The little train depot was from out of the past. In a corner was an old-fashioned telephone booth so Bob called our bed and breakfast. No answer! Bob asked the ticket agent if there is a hotel in town. He said there is one out on the highway about 8 miles away. So how do we get there? "Just call the police station." Soon, there was a Police car and the driver was Luis Coca, Chief of Police!

The Chief gave us a little tour of Rugby and told us to call them in the morning and they would take us to the station to catch the train at 7 a.m.

    Not too far from the Econo Lodge was the monument made of rocks from all over North Dakota to mark this spot as the Center of the North American Continent.

    Much to our delight, there is a museum to visit with a model town circa 1800's erected behind the museum. The old schoolhouse had desks with inkwells like the ones I used as a kid. My husband had dipped my friend Kris' hair in his inkwell. Luckily, her hair was black! But she never forgave him!

There were old sleighs, covered wagons, old cars, a dressmaker, washing machines.

I was disturbed to see a mannequin wearing a 1940's wedding gown. Since I was married in 1947, does that make me an antique? Don't answer that!

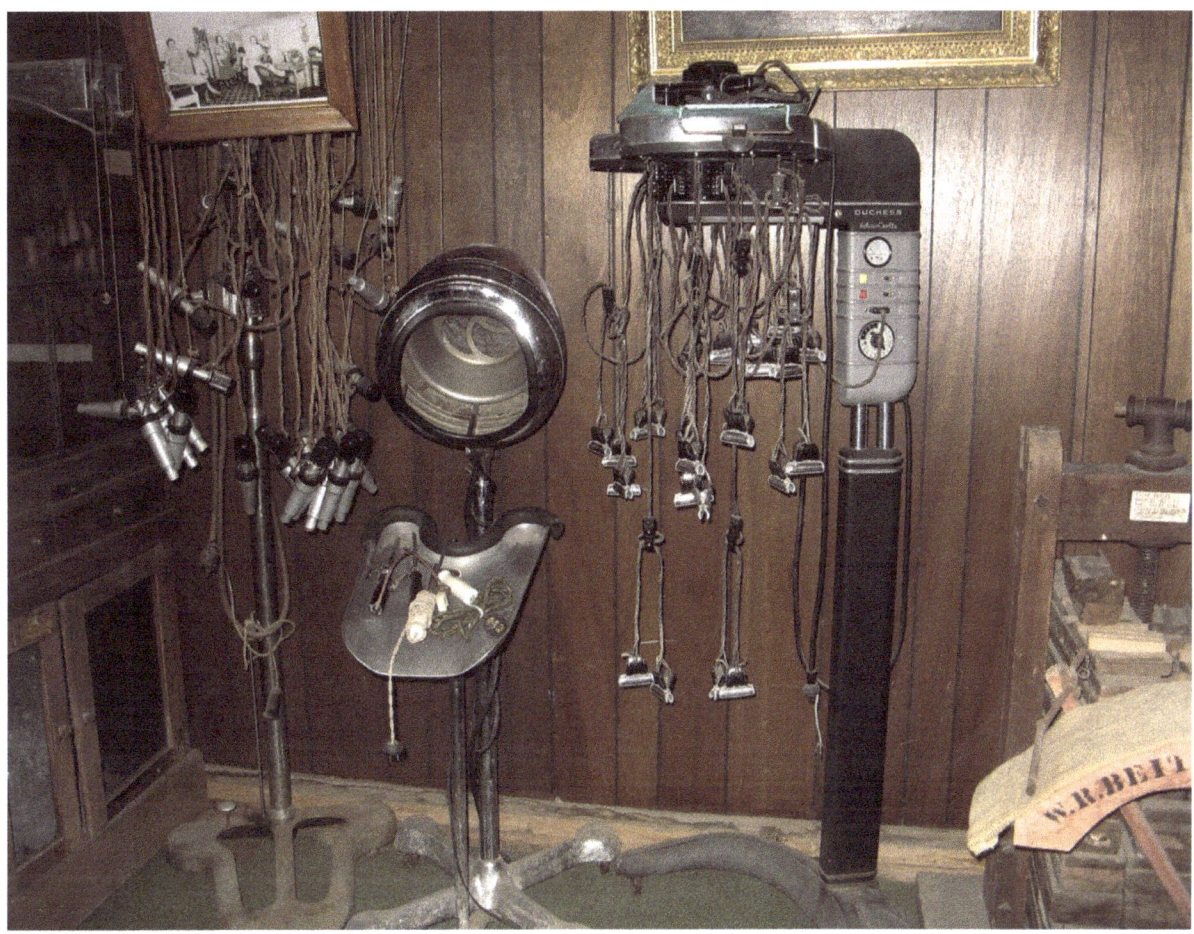

The picture above shows the torture we put up with to have curly hair. Those "things" were clamped on our hair and then heated up to permanently curl our hair. It was called a "permanent" and was the way hair was curled for about 20 years. Unfortunately, all during my young years.

A young police officer took us to the train station in the morning. The train was an hour late, so we visited with a young lady who was meeting a bunch of kids returning from a trip to Chicago. She said, had she known we had no transportation, she would have taken us to see the Peace Park and the winery. What a delightful town! Excellent choice! My goal of 50 states was reached and only one more state to go for Bob: Idaho.

We boarded the "Empire Builder" and spent most of the day in the lounge car with a curved glass ceiling taking pictures of Montana's wide-open spaces.

See what I mean!

We got off the train in Whitefish, Montana, rented a car, and found a motel for the night. Heaven, real beds!

Bob had never been to a ski resort, so, even though it was summer, the next morning, we drove to the Big Mountain Ski Resort and took a gondola to the top 6,817 feet. Riding with us on the gondola were daredevil bikers who would ride their bikes down the ski slopes.

In the summer, they have a ride in this thing pictured above that would take us down the mountain. Bob was willing to try it, but not me, so we took the gondola down. I really liked Bob because he always let me have my way!

A picturesque drive took us around Flathead Lake, the biggest lake west of the Mississippi with mountain peaks on all sides. We were headed for the town of Ronan and a bed and breakfast owned by Mara, a friend we had met in Africa. On a gravel road, we began to climb until we reached a gate and punched in the gate code for entrance to Mandorla Ranch. Mara's husband had built everything with the trees that grew on the property.

We were greeted by Mara and her two dogs, Hobo and Mack. An evening of reminiscing our African adventures was followed by our second good night's sleep since we left Georgia six days ago.

After a many course breakfast, Mara mapped out a day of sightseeing. We visited several Indian museums and had lunch at a drive-in. Can't resist telling you about the huckleberry shake we drank sitting under a big willow tree. As we learned, huckleberries only grow wild and are not easy to find as the bears are well-acquainted with their location and usually find them first.

We drove across the valley to the Bison Range and were able to enter free of charge with our National Park pass. We drove around the 20-mile trip on gravel with a 20-mile-an-hour speed limit, straining our eyes to see wildlife. First, two deer and then some big horn sheep. All at once, a whole hillside of buffalo. Thinking of the old song, "Home on the Range" where the deer and the antelope play … it is a sad reminder that buffalo are confined to a few hillsides when they used to have the freedom of the Old Wild West.

Thank goodness for another good night's sleep and a yummy breakfast shared with a family visiting from England. Meeting new people is why we like B&B's plus the delicious food.

Leaving the ranch, we drove along the opposite side of Flathead Lake past cherry tree orchards and a young lady selling them by the bag! Yum, yum! Loved the signs along the road: Be Polite, Don't Tailgate! I wish they had these signs in Georgia.

Our destination: Glacier National Park. Cars were lined up to enter, but with our pass, we entered with no wait. From the highway, we could see the train tracks we would be riding on later that evening. Lunch in the park was topped off with huckleberry pie and ice cream.

Turning our car in at Whitefish, we were once again aboard the "Empire Builder," and on our way to Bob's 50th State, Idaho. Arriving in Sand Point at midnight, we called our B&B, and soon we were picked up by our hostess, Heather, and put to bed at her Church Street House built in 1915 and placed on the National Registry of Historic Places. And, boy, was that bed welcome! Even more welcome was Heather's breakfast: coffee, orange juice, fruit compote of raspberries, strawberries and blueberries, and an English muffin with creamed spinach and egg sauce on top. You don't get a breakfast like that at a Holiday Inn!

The town was in walking distance and had an interesting "bridge market" that crosses the Pend Oreille River.

We had a cheese beer soup and salad lunch at Mick Duff's accompanied with wheat beer for Bob, huckleberry blond beer for me. Experimenting with new food and drink is half the fun of traveling (maybe three-fourths).

The afternoon couldn't have been better spent than by taking a long nap. My cousin Jean's son Chris' family, who live nearby, picked us up for dinner by a lake. Bob and I split a spearfish dinner and surprise! Huckleberry cheesecake! We didn't split that. Who knows, we may never have huckleberries again.

Our last day in Sand Point, Chris' wife, Kim, and son, Logan, drove us to the top of the local ski mountain. It was cold and rainy (in August?) but that didn't keep us from enjoying our first buffalo burgers with caramelized onions and surprise! Strawberry rhubarb pie and huckleberry ice cream. At dinner time, we walked to Connie's Restaurant and had martinis. Good ones! We toasted our Mission Accomplished as we both had completed our 50-state goal. However, we still had to get home.

We packed and were in bed by 8:30. We (and Heather) set our alarms for 1:45 a.m. She took us to the station (not open at night) and stayed with us until the train came at 2:32 a.m. as it was freezing outside.

We found our roomette #3 with the beds made up. Bob had a heck of a time getting into the upper bunk. I snuggled into bed and thought of a lot of words to describe the motion of the train: jiggly, bumpy, shaky, rocking, bouncing, banging, jerking accompanied by chuck, chuck, chuck in and out of tunnels.

The dining car opened at 6:30 a.m. Our porter couldn't believe we were up already after only four hours of sleep in our roomette torture chamber. We walked through six coach cars to the dining car and sat with a young man from Dallas and a lady from Seattle going to Duluth, Minnesota, for her eighth-grade reunion (1939)! The "seating" porter said we shouldn't be sitting there as the waiter wouldn't get on the train until the train stopped at Whitefish. After a few dissenting words, we stuck to our guns and were "allowed" to keep our seats.

The landscape was solid trees when we saw the obelisk marking 5,216 feet as we crossed the Continental Divide. Shortly, the trees disappeared and rolling grassy hills dominated the Big Sky Country. Clickety clack, clickety clack. Sometimes I felt like a toy being shaken by a dog. Bob and I played solitaire and gin rummy and then another night in our torture chamber. Bob did sleep better, and another day passed as we pulled into Chicago.

We boarded the "City of New Orleans," a 24-car train, in time for dinner. Of course, that meant we had another night in the roomette and a day traveling south. Coming into New Orleans, we passed by the Astrodome where much of New Orleans had slept during the Hurricane Katrina catastrophe. The train station was busy and taxis easy to get.

Our taxi soon found our Place d'Arm on St. Ann and we found our room 125 after passing through gardens, patios, under French balconies and past a fountain.

Heavy wooden shutters covered the windows as well as the door, reminders of Hurricane Katrina. We walked down Bourbon Street to the Red Fish Café. Now, New Orleans is one of the food capitals of the world so I can't miss tell you about this dinner. Bob had jambalaya and I had sweet potato encrusted catfish and wine from Fess Parker's winery in Santa Barbara. Many years ago, much to my kids' delight, Fess Parker, who played Daniel Boone and Davey Crockett on TV, was a guest in our house in Sierra Madre. We couldn't resist trying his wine and the yummy dessert!

The next day we rode the St. Charles streetcar to the end of the line, returning in a pouring rain. We changed into dry clothes and walked to the French Market where I bought an alligator head to go with my stuffed piranha I bought on the Amazon.

Seeing river boats sailing down the river and just walking around New Orleans is a joy as every block or so there is a pick-up band playing New Orleans jazz.

A specialty at the French Market is a beignet (the heart of a donut). Don't leave New Orleans without eating one with a cup of coffee!

Another good dinner on a balcony overlooking Bourbon Street with music drifting from across the way: "Rollin' on the River." A perfect ending and a good night's sleep before boarding the train for home.

The train crossed over miles and miles of Lake Pontchartrain. Kudzu took over until we reached Aniston, Alabama. We jumped off the train, jumped into Bob's car and drove paralleling the tracks and arrived in Villa Rica, just ahead of the train in time to wave as it went by.

The passenger train roars by as the freight train waits on a sidetrack.

Mission accomplished by a couple enjoying their Platinum Years.

Chapter Two
Planning: Around the World in 48 Days
England

Sleep is probably what I do best. I try to say my prayers before I go to sleep, but most of the time, I am asleep before I have asked the Lord to bless all the members of my family and any of my friends who could use some help from the Lord during the coronavirus pandemic. Realizing this some time ago, I begin and end with the list alternating the oldest to the youngest and then the youngest to the oldest. I am very fortunate to have a long list of family and some very good friends.

As soon as I'm horizontal, I am asleep. And much like a horse, I used to sleep standing up on the crowded streetcar coming home from work in Los Angeles when I was 17. I just hung on to the strap and leaned my head against it and slept until the conductor called my street.

As a youngster, a big problem was not being able to stay awake through a whole movie at the theater. I hated not seeing the end! One night, my folks were driving us home from the movies eight blocks away and Daddy parked the car in the garage, and they went into the house. My mom wondered where I was and found me still asleep in the back seat of the car. If my homework wasn't finished by 9 o'clock, forget it!

I do have a talent. I can look at a clock and visualize the hands moving 15 minutes or 2 hours or anytime in between, fall asleep and wake at the time I visualized. This comes in very handy! If I didn't set a time to wake up, I would probably sleep my life away. Eight hours sleep at night is suggested as perfect, so I check the time I retire, add 8 hours and voila! I wake up. Try it!

Planning is what I do second best. My youngest son Tony gave me a computer in 1985, and I soon learned how to make plane and hotel reservations. One word of warning: it is best to contact the actual hotel or B&B and not trust a "travel" company. One exception to that rule was our trip to Africa, so well planned by Unchartered Outposts headquartered in Santa Fe. Bob always said that Africa is the only place he would go back to. (Forgive ending in a preposition.)

My early Platinum Years with Bob were peppered with a cruise on the Mediterranean from Barcelona to Greece, Argentina to Manaus on the Amazon River, and Amsterdam to Budapest on the Danube. These trips are recorded in my book "*Grossly Outnumbered*," published when I was 85. That book ended with the desire to take a trip around the world and the planning began!

Bob and I had enough frequent flyer miles to do Delta's Around the World plan with six stops, always proceeding in one direction, no backtracking, for only $500 for airport taxes. Choosing the six stops was the heart of the "planning." We settled on England (Scotland), Egypt, India, Bali, and Australia, often transferring through Korea. Delta's partners also figured in the planning. Making the reservations 100 days in advance, a problem did arise two weeks before we were scheduled to leave. Air France cancelled their flights from Egypt to India. This was very important because we had to be in New Delhi to catch a train on a certain date.

A two-hour phone call to a helpful and persistent Delta representative finally solved the problem with a crazy flight plan: Cairo to Nairobi to Uganda to Amsterdam to New Delhi on Delta partner KLM. At this time, I was in my 88th year, and I needed all my computer skills to arrange B&B's in all these countries. England was easy as I had a friend Jimmy and I had met in Fairfield years ago who lived near Oxford. Jimmy and I had stayed with Barbara Day in 1999 and she welcomed Bob and me in 2012.

We would ride the train into London each day, ride the big red bus and do the tourist things. Riding the Eye was Bob's first choice.

    One day, on the way back to Oxford, I noticed that a big nuclear power plant was on the wrong side of the train. I asked the conductor if we were going to Oxford. He said, "No, madam, we are going to Wales. You need to get off at Swindon and go back and start over."

    Swindon rang a bell in my conscience. When No. 1 Son Jim was in junior high school, all students had to do a 7th grade science project. That would have been easy for Jon, Jac or Tony, but Jim was not into science. The project he created was to test the pH factor in soil from around the world. He sent sandwich size plastic bags to many countries in the world as well as the states in the U.S. requesting an ounce of soil. Realizing he might be dealing with agricultural restrictions, he addressed his requests to mayors of towns.

For the next few months, it was exciting receiving these envelopes from all over the world. Russia was one country that did not reply. The secretary to the mayor from a town in Spain replied she had gathered the soil from the most famous bull ring nearby! The reply from Alaska was a note saying the ground was frozen and the mayor had to dig under his house to get the soil. And Maine was so proud of its soil it sent a box with a big dirt clod full of weeds.

So, why did Swindon ring a bell? Many British folks had moved to Sierra Madre because there was a British Home for retired British subjects. They had brought the sport of soccer to our town and Tony and Jac enjoyed participating. One day, one of the soccer moms came to our door and showed me her hometown paper from Swindon, England. The headline, AN OUNCE OF SWINDON GOES TO THE U.S.A.

Bob took a picture of me under the Swindon sign and we eventually found our way to Oxford and a nice dinner with Barbara Day at a local pub. The next day Barbara drove us through the narrow hedgerows to Blenheim Palace where Winston Churchill was born. Hard to imagine anyone growing up in such an enormous place.

This was our last day with Barbara as we gathered our stuff together the next morning and headed for King's Cross Station. We checked our big bags and boarded the train for Scotland.

We transferred trains at the Haymarket Station where a charming Scotsman, dressed in kilts to attend a wedding, helped us get on the right train for St. Andrews.

Note the silver angel on my jacket. It has protected me on all trips, especially airplane flights.

Since planning is what I do second best, the computer came in handy again as I looked up Bed and Breakfasts in St. Andrews, Scotland. I discovered Scots Craig B&B and made reservations. Our hosts, Moira and Richard Burns, met us at the train and provided us with a comfy bedroom and breakfast in their sunny garden room. Bob's curiosity made him try blood sausage and haggis made from kidneys and who knows what all. I stuck to bacon and eggs, blackberries, strawberries and kiwi compote, porridge and toast.

I grew up calling porridge, "mush." This reminded me of the old nursery rhyme: Peas porridge hot, Peas porridge cold, Peas porridge in the pot, nine days old.

Of course, being golfers, we headed for St. Andrews Golf Course. We knew it was closed on Sunday (too expensive, anyway!). However, anyone can walk around the course and the Himalaya Putting Course is open on Sunday. Correctly named, it is up and down hills with long putts.

Lunch at a local hotel provided another interesting menu. I warmed up with finan haddie (?) soup and Bob had soup with leek, mushrooms, neeps and tatties (turnips and potatoes in Scotch brogue).

Another night with Moira and Richard and, fortified with their delicious breakfast, we again boarded the train for London and Heathrow Airport. We stayed at the Yotel inside the airport as we had a 7 a.m. Air France flight to Egypt via Paris. The room was so small, we had to check our bags outside. If you are looking for luxury, Yotel isn't it!

Chapter Three
Egypt

Our tours in Egypt were arranged by Blue Danube Holidays, a tour company I found on the internet. We were met at the airport and driven through the incredible city of Cairo where there are no traffic lights, and cars fight at every intersection to get through. At the time, warned by our State Department Cairo was dangerous, we stayed on the other side of the Nile River at the beautiful Mena House Oberoi Lodge. My No. 4 son Jac had recommended it and it was very luxurious—quite a contrast to Yotel! Originally this was a hunting lodge.

      Settled in, we headed for the dining room. I asked the host, where are the pyramids from here? He pointed toward the window. Looking through the beaded curtains in the dining room, we could see the huge Giza pyramid. WOW!

Every room was beautiful including the bar where we could get good martinis!

Our guide would meet us every morning after breakfast and he, with the driver, would take us to see all the sights. Very soon we realized that everything in Egypt is BIG! As you can see, the stones of the great Giza pyramid were as tall as me.

Behind the big pyramid were smaller pyramids for lesser pharaohs.

Even more amazing was looking one direction across the Nile and seeing the huge City of Cairo and looking the other direction and seeing nothing but desert and two camels off in the distance.

The sphinx was our next stop. Yes, everything in Egypt is BIG!

Our days seeing the antiquities passed quickly. Then another wild trip back to the airport and we were flying to Aswan Dam on the River Nile.

George, our new guide, gave us a boat tour on the river showing us where the dam had flooded many islands with gigantic monuments (below) that have been reconstructed on another island when the water reached full capacity in 1976.

All the Egyptian ladies show their belly buttons!

George took us to a huge quarry on the outskirts of Aswan from whence came the famous obelisks now standing in London. Rome and Paris. It was 105 degrees and he is asking us to climb up this rock to see the unfinished obelisk?

We did it and here it is. Proof positive!!

Finally, George took us to our ship for our cruise down the Nile.

It was certainly not a 5-star ship as billed. We were the only English speaking aboard apart from a couple and their young son from Wales. The passengers were French or German, neither very friendly. We realized we had not seen an American tourist on this whole trip.

Spending most of our time on the top deck, we enjoyed watching the activity along the shore. Looking at civilization on the edge of the river, and, beyond, the empty desert sand spread to the edge of the horizon.

Our guide, George, followed the boat and met us at each port and spent the day taking us to see the wonders of ancient Egypt.

Entering an ancient tomb on this hillside, (no pictures allowed) the paintings on the walls were as fresh as if painted that very day.

At Karnak, we visited the famous Avenue of the Sphinxes.

At Luxor, we visited a tomb in the Valley of the Kings and the spectacular Temple of Queen Hatshepsut.

Then it was time to say goodbye to George and fly back to Cairo arriving at midnight. What a day!

And we are looking at 48 hours without a bed! The best laid plans of mice and men! Then came the crazy patchwork route to India that the Delta agent figured out. Kenya Airways flew us from Cairo to Nairobi, landing in Khartoum, Sudan, in the middle of the night to pick up passengers en route. We changed flights in Nairobi and flew to Entebbe, Uganda, for a 15-hour layover before a KLM flight to Amsterdam and finally India.

Nearing Entebbe, we landed beside Lake Victoria, the source of the Nile River. Unfortunately, the State Department had warned us it was too dangerous to leave the airport in Entebbe, so we were stuck in the KLM lounge for our 15-hour layover. It was worth the $30 charge as it provided showers and food and couches to sleep on … and I did sleep a solid 8 hours!

    The first flight took us to Amsterdam with a layover just long enough to trek around the airport before boarding another plane for New Delhi, India.

Chapter Four
India

On our arrival in New Delhi, we were welcomed by Roy, a representative for the Palace on Wheels.

He drove us to our B&B I had scheduled on the internet. The big hotels in India had been bombed recently so I figured the bombers wouldn't bother to bomb a B&B. Mega Homestay was a four-story building, but our very nice room was on the main floor. The next day, a driver took us sightseeing including Humayun's Tomb that was the inspiration for the Taj Mahal. At 4:30 p.m., a small band welcomed us aboard the Palace on Wheels for our 8-day train ride through the Rajasthan part of India.

In 1999, my son, Jim, and I met in India. He was travelling around the world coming from Vietnam and knew I had always wanted to see India and that my husband didn't. On that trip, we did bus tours and flew to Katmandu, Nepal. Jim had no liking for India, but I was fascinated. Planning this trip with Bob, with our bedroom and bathroom on the train, was a much more luxurious way of seeing India.

The train was truly a palace with every comfort including two dining rooms, a spa coach, and a bar with martinis available. All our needs were attended to by our two butlers, Umesh and Pradash. Always at our beck and call, they never complained when I often accidentally pushed their call button instead of the light switch.

The train traveled at night while we slept in our comfortable beds, and, each day, we were in a new location with much to see. I was always overwhelmed by the intricate designs in Indian architecture. The peacock is often used as is the Hindu God, Ganesh, an elephant who removes obstacles. Of course, the elephant is my favorite animal as exhibited by my large collection of elephants and a small one I always wear on a chain around my neck. I hate to admit I am a little superstitious as I also knock on wood if I boast untimely about my good fortune.

Never missing an opportunity to ride an elephant, Bob and I rode a gaily painted elephant up to the Amber Fort, a fabulous example of Mughal designs.

You know my love of elephants, so I was pleased to see the elephant with arms in the middle of the entrance to the fort. He is Ganesh, the God who removes obstacles.

Women had a separate part of the fort. The picture above is a kind of "window" for them to see the beautiful gardens in the next picture and they can't be seen.

Now you see what I mean about the Mughal designs.

Bob and I saw many more forts built on the top of mountains. Jaiselmer was my favorite. When our fellow travelers looked at this climb, they were hesitant to do it until they saw Bob and me start up. They said if we old folks could do it, they would.

Here, as all over India, you see the belief that cows are sacred. Our driver told us that if you hit a cow on the highway, it is very bad karma!

    We were allowed to visit the Patwon Ji ki Haveli, the most important and largest haveli (mansion). It was the first erected in Jaisalmer. Constructed in the year 1805 by Guman Chand Patwa, he was then a rich trader of jewelry and fine brocades. Completed in the span of 50 years, Patwon Ji Ki is renowned for its ornate wall paintings, and intricate yellow sandstone-carved jharokhas (balconies), gateways, and archways. I am surprised it took only 50 years to do this carving.

      I should tell you that you do need to watch your step not to step on a cow "pie". The Indian people (I should say women) gather these "pies" to recycle and use for firewood, to patch roofs and other uses.

My second visit to the Taj Mahal was no less spectacular. Built of marble and inlaid with jewels, it is without question, the most beautiful building in the world. It should be seen at dawn and sunset.

The previous picture shows how the jewels are set in the marble. The Taj Mahal is literally covered with these jewels. Built in Agra between 1631 and 1648 by order of the Mughal emperor, Shah Jahan, in memory of his favorite wife. Sha Jahan planned to build a copy of the Taj across the river in black marble for his own tomb.

An early morning wakeup took us to Bharatpur Bird Sanctuary which had been a hunting place for Rajahs and their friends. Listed on a big wood marker were the totals of birds shot by famous people (British officers and royalty) on recorded dates starting in 1902. One hunt listed 4,000 birds killed. Now we were able to enjoy this peaceful spot riding quietly in a bicycle rickshaw. Our knowledgeable driver was 60 years old.

It was so quiet and peaceful with beautiful birds flying around and other wildlife including monkeys. Afterwards we had a lovely dinner at a Maharajah's palace.

We made some lovely friends aboard the train. Barbara and Francisco Chan, below, were so helpful to Bob and me. Sometimes we were climbing on high bridges over train tracks and Barbara always gave me a hand. Francisco helped Bob figure out how to get money out of the ATM machines.

Now living in South Carolina, this sweet couple have visited me in Georgia and gave me an elephant for my collection. The couple on the left were from Australia.

After eight nights sleeping as we rolled along, our last night in India was again at Megha Homestay.

Greeted by our host Arman and his mother, our room was ready. Arman suggested a lovely restaurant for martinis and dinner. Most welcome as restaurants in India usually do not serve alcohol.

Then it was goodbye to our host Arman and to India.

Chapter Five
Bali

Our next flight was to Bali, Indonesia, by way of Korea, of course! Leaving New Delhi at 00:45 a.m. Yes, the middle of the night! Again, our plans went awry as our flight was delayed until 1:38 a.m. so we missed our 6 a.m. connection in Guangzhou, China. We spent the day in the empty airport looking out the window at the boarding bridge and no plane. The local crew, speaking no English, did not know what to do with us. Finally, they brought us a box lunch like they were eating. This delay also caused us to miss our flight from Seoul, Korea, to Bali and to have one less day in Bali. Korean Airlines are partners with Delta and provide most flights in Asia so using Delta means to go anywhere in Asia, one must go through Korea first.

Korea does have a very modern airport and they kindly arranged for a hotel nearby to spend the night before our 6 p.m. flight to Bali. I tried to use the computer to notify the B&B in Bali we would be arriving at midnight a day later than scheduled. Everything on the computer was in Korean, so Delta was kind enough to call them the next morning.

"Computer literate Ginny" had arranged for a seven night stay at the Matahari Cottage B&B located an hour from the airport in Ubud, Bali. Planning on the computer, it looked fascinating with each room being a separate cottage and each cottage with a different theme. Since the Japanese style one meant sleeping on the floor, I chose the Barong cottage. This was a perfect place to relax from all the structured sightseeing we had been doing for weeks.

Bali is Hawaii in triplicate. Our cottage was nestled in a veritable paradise of tropical plants and trees. Our front porch had a peekaboo view of the pool and breakfast deck. The disappearing edge swimming pool was truly disappearing into a ravine so deep and full of vegetation that one could not see the bottom.

I loved looking up at the high, pointed bamboo ceiling of our cottage. A beautiful hand-painted door led to our outdoor bathroom with a sunken tub and marble shower and a high bamboo fence enclosed tropical garden. Bob and I had forgotten to pack shorts. Darling Iluh, our hostess, went to the local market and brought us each a pair of shorts and a funny top for me.

Our front porch with a view of the pool through the tropical vegetation.

Breakfast was served by the pool. Lunch and dinner were within walking distance and couldn't have been more delicious as we had not had any fresh vegetables in Egypt or India. While eating at Bali Buddha, we could hear a chicken cackling. How fresh is that??

Our favorite nighttime dining was at Nomad, an indoor-outdoor restaurant two blocks away. The owner greeted us by placing plumeria flowers behind Bob's and my ears. Satay is chicken on a stick and became a favorite of ours. Nomad also served the best dry martinis! We loved sitting where we could watch the activity on the street, people carrying the most amazing things on their heads, pots and even a table. Across the street was a Ralph Lauren store and a fancy lace negligee shop. If a man and woman went into the negligee shop, I watched to see if the woman was lucky enough to come out with a purchase. I wasn't! Too expensive!

Iluh's cousin, Dewa, was the one who came at midnight to the airport two nights in a row to pick us up. On his and her day off, they drove us around to see all the interesting sights, the monkey forest, waterfalls, rice paddies, wood carvers and where they make batik clothing. Next, they drove us up a ridge just wide enough for a narrow road with severe drop off on both sides until we got to the top. All the while, the three volcanoes were smoking across an enormous valley.

At the top was a lovely restaurant cantilevered over steep terrain so thick with vegetation, the houses barely peeked out. We were served delicious fish satay and introduced to many strange fruits. Iluh showed us how to eat mangostim.

And then it was off to a coffee plantation. Traveling through the countryside, the road was lined with flowering poinsettias and roadside stands. The plantation was on the side of a steep slope and the family grew all kinds of fruit as well as coffee and spices. We were served eight different drinks: ginger tea, chocolate, cinnamon tea, ginseng tea and fresh coconut milk and several kinds of coffee. Coffee beans were being roasted by a 94-year-old woman still going strong in her Platinum Years.

Two interesting things about Bali are every block has a Buddhist temple and all houses are behind walls … not visible from the street. On our street, I could see an elephant statue through the doorway of the temple. I finally had the nerve one day to go inside. The elephant had a crown and was holding his Hindu symbols of protection, the axe and the lotus blossom. Our street also had a post office with free picture postcards and a dress shop with smiley ladies sewing lovely dresses. They always laughed and waved at us when we went by, probably because we were good customers.

On one of our touring days, Iluh took us inside the wall to see her house. I should say houses as there were four separate buildings: north, east, south and west. The south building is their living quarters. The kitchen building was set apart and a few chickens were walking around. One building was like an open pavilion where they have celebrations and another building was in a lovely garden where they pray and give offerings. The architectural details and curved roof lines reflected an Oriental influence, a favorite of mine.

We met Iluh's family and were served tea and goodies and then it was off to my seventh elephant ride. I love being as high as an elephant's eye. However, at the end of the ride, our mahout told me to climb on Laura's head, which I did willingly until he told me we were going to do some tricks. I said, "No thanks" and climbed onto the ramp.

Bob. on the other hand, agreed and sat on Laura's head. Thinking he was alone on the elephant, he got very nervous when the elephant started performing and he thought he was going to fall off. He was unaware the mahout was on the elephant sitting right behind him

    Six fantastic days in this island paradise where no one will ever go hungry as there are always bananas and coconuts overhead. It took an afternoon to fit all our stuff and all the new stuff into our luggage. Dewa picked us up at 9 p.m. for our flight at 1:30 a.m. We shipped three bags through to Sydney as we had a nine-hour layover in Seoul. We dozed and read for seven hours and unlike our last arrival in Korea, this one was a real treat!

Chapter Six
Korea

This scheduled stay in Korea for nine hours made it possible for me to contact Mr. and Mrs. Yi by e-mail before we left on this trip. I met this couple when I visited Korea in the 1970's. My son, Jim, and Mr. Yi were co-teachers of English in Korea while Jim served three years in the Peace Corps.

My whole life I had wanted to visit Japan, but when I finally visited Tokyo lit up with a million neon signs, I was so disappointed. On the other hand, Korea in the 1970's was the quiet landscape I had always visualized. Little thatched roof villages looking like little mushroom caps amongst the rice fields. Seoul was a two-story town with one modern six-story hotel. The rest of the country slept on the floor and I loved it!

When Bob and I arrived at the new airport in Incheon, Mr. and Mrs. Yi met us with a big welcoming sign.

They had driven a long way from Taigu, leaving their home at 3 a.m. Their son, Wangi (a baby when I first saw him in Andong, a few hundred miles south of Seoul) had arranged a lunch for us at a beautiful traditional Korean restaurant in the old part of Seoul. Poor Mr. Yi, unfamiliar with Seoul, had a difficult time finding it. No longer a two-story town, Seoul had towering skyscrapers, thanks to their huge growth when they hosted the Olympics in 1988.

Mr. Yi said because we had so little time, it would be a light lunch. I lost count as course after course arrived: raw fish, cooked fish, beef, onions, cabbage, seaweed, duck, blue berries, pineapple, many soups, fried rice, special tea and on and on. The long table was full, even though the waitress kept clearing. Each dish was a work of art and Bob was loving it, showing how adept he was with chopsticks. Bob had installed a computer system in Okinawa many years before and learned how to eat with chopsticks.

When Jim was doing his round the world flight and I met him in India, he had flown west from Boston, as opposed to our round the world flight flying east. His first stop was San Francisco, then Korea and Vietnam, before meeting me in India. It had been twenty-four years since Jim had been in the hotel in Seoul. A young man stopped him and asked: "Are you Chu Im Su?" (Jim's Korean name) "I was in your 7th grade class in Andong." Now 41, he was teaching English Literature at the university and had received a PhD in American Literature, his thesis on Mark Twain.

A few years later, the Yi's visited me in Georgia. They flew to Boston to visit Jim and then to Atlanta to visit me. They presented me with a traditional Korean kimono complete with shoes!

At our farewell to the Yi's in the new airport in Inchon, they loaded us down with ginseng tea and an umbrella and an invitation to come back for a longer visit. We were scheduled for another 10-hour flight to Sydney, Australia.

Chapter Seven
Australia

My son, Jim, arrived in Sydney the day before we did, so he met us when we arrived at 6 a.m. Jim teaches classes every summer in Australia. By the way, he and I have a running competition of countries visited. However, I have bragging rights in that I have visited all the continents now that I have been to Australia. He has not been on the African continent.

Jim's generous friends, Brian and Grant, live on Goodlet Lane in Sydney. I mention this because the Aussies often use quaint names. They moved in with nearby friends so we could use their home for our three days in Sydney. When Jim served us breakfast, I thought it odd because I thought it was dinner time! That is what jet travel does to you.

Jim, always the veritable tour guide, took us to Sydney Harbor and a cup of coffee to warm our bones as our summer is their winter. We toured the Sydney Opera House, certainly a most complicated architectural achievement. It looks like a series of shells sitting in the water

And just beyond a big Princess Cruise ship was sailing under the harbor bridge.

Brian and Grant drove us to the magnificent Blue Mountains in the afternoon where we saw the Three Sisters, a rock formation joined by bridges.

Returning to Sydney, Bob and I realized on this whole trip around the world, we were never in a country which drove on the right side of the road proving: "The sun never set on the British Empire."

Our second day, we bought a $21 ticket that took us anywhere on all transportation for 24 hours. We bussed to downtown and spent the entire day getting on and off ferries to different parts of this enormous bay full of islands. The ferries are the main transportation for the people to get from their island homes.

Our last ferry ride of the day took us to the mouth of this huge bay where surfers were enjoying the waves. After a glass of wine and snack at a waterfront café, Jim and Bob decided to check the temperature of the water.

A wave caught them by surprise and they both went down. Bob got the worst of it and, unfortunately, had to ride the ferry all the way back soaking wet. Not only was he soaked and full of sand, but his wallet was completely ruined.

I, on the other hand, enjoyed a nap.

Next day, we visited Jim's favorite store, the very elegant David Jones, with clerks who actually greeted you with "How may I help you?" How long since you have been waited on in a department store?

Actually, David Jones is really two stores across the street from each other: one for women and one for men connected at the basement level, a lovely market.

Since Bob's wallet was ruined by the wave, we found out our dollar isn't worth much as the cheapest wallet was $99.

I am hard pressed not to tell you about our last dinner in Sydney, so suffice it to say I wrote down each course including the five desserts in my journal. The next morning, Jim joined us as we boarded a train and traveled through sparse farmland for 12 hours on our way to Melbourne.

My early planning on the internet had found a 125-year-old Victoria Hotel in Melbourne. My past experiences had proved that old hotels have much bigger rooms and nicer accommodations. This hotel proved to be close to everything as the public transportation is phenomenal.

It was only a short walk to breakfast at the CoffeeEx, very delicious and almost worth the $18 price tag. Already realizing that Australia's economy was considerably higher than ours, I later was forced into buying a pair of shoes for $160 as one of my shoes turned up missing. Probably under the bed in Bali.

Bob cleaned his plate or should I say "plates".

Many of the city's sights were within walking distance. Our first destination was the magnificent Aboriginal Museum where we saw some awesome folk art. Some were spiritually mesmerizing while others featured animals and sea life.

Very soon, as we approached the huge library, we became aware of the Aussies' sense of humor. There are many lovely reading rooms and displays surrounding the main hall. We saw a 1788 map of the United States with Florida having a very strange shape. I was fascinated with a Rajasthan Indian painting of Alexander the Great's flying machine: Griffins were pulling Alexander up. He was holding meat just beyond their reach.

One big tourist attraction is the "tallest building in the Southern Hemisphere." This building offers the "Edge" where we could have walked out onto a glass platform on the top floor. The floor was wavy on purpose to make you feel dizzy and I did. The middle building is the edge.

It seems Jim has friends everywhere as we had lunch with a lady friend of his and then afternoon tea with Sister Mary Ann. Our last night in Melbourne, we were invited to a fabulous Dinner-Recital given by Jim's friend Kevin Meese. Other guests were Kevin's friend from India, his mother, his sister and a girl from England.

Between courses, Kevin played his Steinway grand piano. Tchaikovsky's "Prelude" with the hors d'oeuvres. Brahms accompanied the entre, lamb in sauce with parsnips, carrots and onions. Mozart accompanied the spectacular billowy blueberry meringue made by his mother.

What a climax to our stay in Sydney! I make no apologies for describing this meal.

Chapter Eight
Anglesea

Our next few days in Australia, we enjoyed meeting and spending time with Jim's friends, Rose and Ross Dennis. They picked us up at the Victoria Hotel and drove us to their vacation house in a beach community called Anglesea.

More Aussie humor!

Bob and a little Aussie humor of his own!

Their house was on Bogey Ct, identifying this as a golfing community.

It was obvious that all the birds in the area knew Rose had arrived as they began flying around her the minute she stepped out of the car with bird seed in hand. She gave me a handful of seed and, immediately, birds were eating out of my hand!

And that is not just an expression. They were perched on the porch railing and really eating out of my hand. Some had red bellies and green wings, and some had red bellies and blue wings and there were beautiful white cockatoos.

Rose not only fed the birds, but it seemed like she fed us non-stop, starting with tea and goodies. Then wine and hors d'oeuvres and a delicious dinner I hate to miss telling you about.

The next morning, Bob and I played golf with kangaroos. I am not kidding as they were hopping across the fairways paying no attention to us. When we finished 18 holes, it was so much fun, we played another 9 holes.

We all went back to the clubhouse for dinner and I took a picture of their entrance sign. I wish our club enforced these great rules, especially regarding no mobile phones and the instructions for children.

The next morning, we were taken to the Great Ocean Road that starts in Anglesea and travels 244 kilometers westward. The road is two lanes with many signs reminding tourists Australians drive on the left side of the road.

Construction on the road began September 1919 and was built by approximately 3,000 returning servicemen as a war memorial for fellow servicemen who had been killed in World War I. In 1924 (an auspicious year as it was the year I was born), a steamboat hit a reef and became stranded near the construction area. The crew was forced to jettison 500 barrels of beer and 120 cases of whiskey. The workers obtained the cargo, resulting in an unscheduled two-week-long drinking break. That was a pretty big celebration of my birth year.

Now we were on our quest to see the elusive koala bear. The first signs are eucalyptus trees completely bare of their leaves. As we came to trees with leaves still intact, we spotted six munching along the branches. In this year of 2020, it is devastating to think of the horrible fires that destroyed so many koala bears and kangaroos, and their habitat.

On this drive, another sign reminded me of Aussie humor:

NO PARKING! CARS WILL BE SHREDDED AND MADE INTO BEER CANS

All too soon our Anglesea visit was over. We packed our bags and we all headed for the Geelong Airport, stopping for lunch at the Ocean Corner Café. I mention this, not because of the food (we did try kangaroo steak) but because it was there I saw the most intriguing water saving toilet. I was already aware of the conscious effort Australians make to save water when I saw a water-saving tank outside the Denis' house and a huge water-saving tank at the house next door.

This toilet at the restaurant has a sink on top of the water tank where you wash your hands and the used water goes back into the water tank. How simple and practical!

And then, it was farewell to our new friends Rose and Dennis Ross and my son Jim, who was staying a while longer in Australia.

Jet Star, our eighth airline on this trip around the world, flew us back to a sunset-lit Sydney. Looking down at the many islands in this big bay, it was easy to see how big a part the ferries play in the daily life of the city dwellers. In this picture I took as we were coming in for a landing, the bridge is visible on the left.

Just to the right of the bridge you can see the opera house.

A night at an airport hotel with a 4 a.m. wakeup call got us to our flight to … Korea! Aren't you surprised? This is the first of two flights it would take to get us to Los Angeles, 21 hours later. My cousin, Jean, had dinner ready for us and a much-needed bed for our 24-hour stayover. My No. 2 son, Jon, drove us to LAX for our last leg.

Four more hours in the air on Delta completed our 48-day circumnavigation of the globe and into the loving arms of my daughter-in-law, Jessie and my No. 5 son, Tony.

Mission accomplished by two senior citizens in their Platinum Years, 86 and 88 years old.

If we had lost our itinerary I prepared on the computer, we would have been lost!

#	FROM	TO	DAY	DATE	AIRLINE	FLT/SEAT	AIR TIME	DEPARTS	ARRIVE	MILES	SPECIAL	HOTEL-B&B
	ITINERARY FOR GINNY AND BOBS AROUND THE WORLD IN 48 DAYS GRAND TOUR 2012											
	ATLANTA	LONDON	MON	MAR 26	DELTA	D10-34F & G	8H 25M	10:45 PM	12:15 PM	4,208	CONFIRMATION: G4Z82D	BARBARA DAY'S
1	LONDON	SCOTLAND	SAT	MAR 31	EAST COAST TRAIN	D 45,46A		12 NOON	6:12 PM		LEAVE KINGS CROSSING	SCOTSCRAIG B&B
	SCOTLAND	LONDON	MON	APR 2	EAST COAST TRAIN	E 56,57A		11:45 AM	5:56 PM		TRANSFER / EDINGURGH	YOTEL-HEATHROW
	LONDON	PARIS	TUE	APR 3	AIR FRANCE	1681	1HR 15M	10:10 AM	12:25 PM	214	'SEATS AT CHECK-IN	
	PARIS	CAIRO	TUE	APR 3	AIR FRANCE	508 31A	4HR 25M	1:35 PM	6:00 PM	1,996	HR. 10 LAYOVER IN PARIS	MENA HOUSE
		CAIRO	WED	APR 4							TOUR PYRAMIDS	MENA HOUSE
2	CAIRO	ASWAN	TH	APR 5	EGYPT AIR	MS391	1 HR 25 M	8:25 AM	9:45 AM		TOUR ASWAN	
	ASWAN			APR 5	BOARD SHIP						3-DAY NILE CRUISE	ABOARD SHIP
	ASWAN	LUXOR	SAT	APR 7								
	LUXOR	CAIRO	SUN	APR 8	EGYPT AIR	MS364	1HR 10M	6:20 PM	7:30 PM			
	CAIRO	NAIROBI	SUN	APR 8	KENYA AIRWAYS	321		11:25PM	6:45 AM	10,593	1 HR. 15M LAYOVER	
	NAIROBI	UGANDA	MON	APR 9	KENYA AIRWAYS	410		7:55 AM	9:10AM		1 HR 15M LAYOVER	
	UGANDA	AMSTERDAM		APR 9	KLM ROYAL DUTCH	537 21A,B		11:30 PM	6:50 PM		14HR 20M LAYOVER	KLM LOUNGE?
	AMSTERDAM	DELHI	TUE	APR 10	KLM ROYAL DUTCH	871 17A,C		11:30 AM	10:50 PM		APRL 10 AND APRIL 18	MEGA HOMESTAY
3	DELHI		WED	APR 11	PALACE ON WHEELS	TRAIN	APR 11-18	4:30 PM			8 DAY 7 NITE TRAIN TRIP.	JAIPUR,UDAIPUR, AGRA
			TUE	APR 18	DELHI CITY TOUR			7:00 AM			RANTHAMBOR, JAISALMER	JODHPUR, TAJ MAHAL
	DELHI	GUANGZHOU	THU	APR 19	CHINA SOUTHERN	360 41 A,C	5H 20M	10:45 PM	6:30 AM	2,264	ARR APR 20 -2HR 30MIN LAYOVER	
	GUANGZHOU	SEOUL-INCHEON	FRI	APR 20	CHINA SOUTHERN	337 39 J,H	3H 15M	9:10 AM	1:15 PM	1,289		
	SEOUL	DENPASSAR, BALI		APR 20	KOREAN AIR	629 39 A,B	7H	6:05 PM	12:05 AM	3,284	MIDNIGHT OF APRIL 21	MATAHARI B&B
4	BALI	SEOUL-INCHEON	SAT	APR 28	KOREAN AIR	630 49 A,B	7H 5M	1:20 AM	9:25 AM	3,284	9 1/2 HOUR LAYOVER IN SEOUL	MET BY MR YI
	SEOUL	SYDNEY	SAT	APR 28	KOREAN AIR	121 39 G,H	10H 10M	7:10 PM	6:20 AM	5,177	ARRIVING SUN, APR 29	BRIAN & GRANT'S
		MELBOURNE			TRAIN							
5	SYDNEY	SEOUL-INCHEON	FRI	MAY 11	KOREAN AIR	122 39 B,C	10H 25M	7:55 AM	5:20 PM	5,177	2 HR 40 MIN LAYOVER	
6	SEOUL	LOS ANGELES		MAY 11	KOREAN AIR	11 48 B,C	11H	8:00 PM	3:00 PM	5,957	1 HR LAYOVER	ARRIVING MAY 11
	LOS ANGELES	ATLANTA	SAT	MAY 12	DELTA		4H 26M	2:45 PM	9:58 PM	1,940	24 HR LAYOVER IN L.A.	COUSIN JEAN'S
							TOTAL	95.25 HRS	4 DAYS	45,383		

If you haven't seen enough pictures of this trip and food, there are even more on my website Tony helped me put together.

aroundtheworldin48days.com

Chapter Nine
Vietnam and Cambodia

Once the travel bug bites you, it is hard not to be planning another trip, so it wasn't long before the bug bit us again. It was 2015 and I celebrated my 91st birthday cruising on the Mekong River with Bob. This added Cambodia and Vietnam to my "Countries Visited List".

Unfortunately, the first day in Hanoi, I fell climbing into a bicycle tuk tuk, landing on my head, but we continued on down a very busy street to see the puppet show. Bob, riding behind me, took this picture of the back of my head and driver's hand.

My driver carried me on his back into the puppet show which was very enjoyable.

My fellow travelers insisted that I go to the hospital when we returned to the hotel. X-rays were taken and verified I had broken some little bones in my foot.

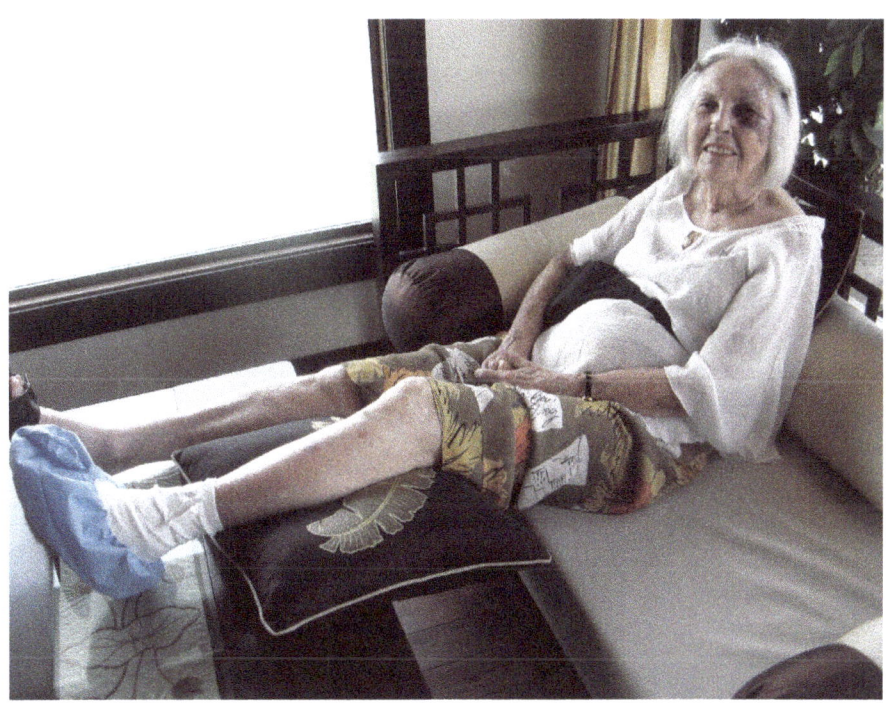

I was able to get around on crutches and we boarded a small ship the next day and sailed the beautiful Halong Bay surrounded by pointed mountains poking up from the bay all around us.

Next, we flew to Cambodia to board our ship for the trip down the Mekong River. But first we had a few days in a magnificent hotel or rather, Bob did.

Unfortunately, I first had to report to the local hospital.

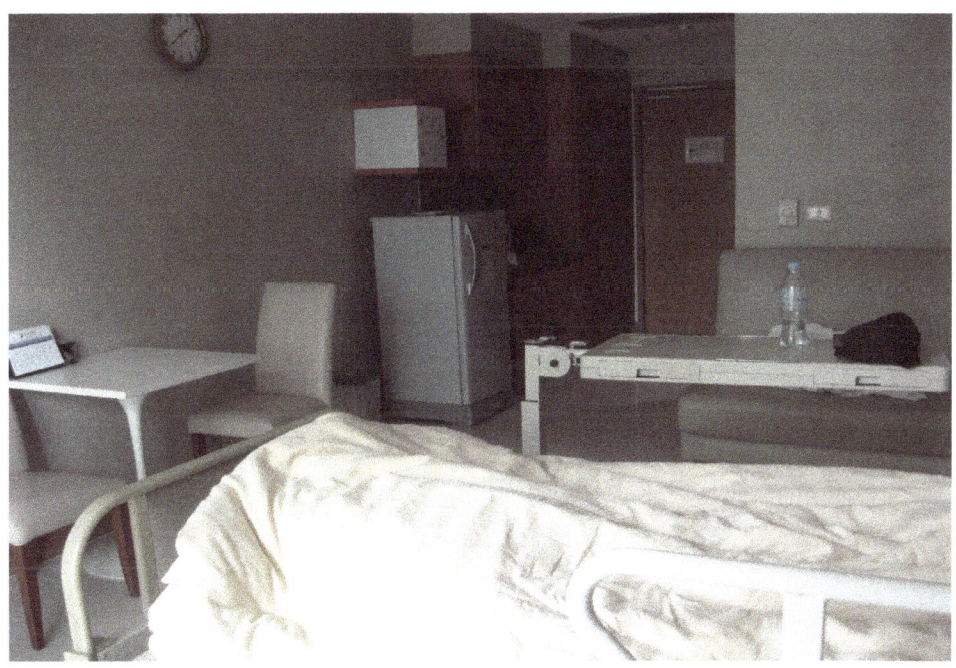

My room was quite comfortable with a couch for Bob to rest, a refrigerator and a lovely balcony with a view of thick vegetation. The food was delicious. The doctor wanted me to stay for three days, but I needed a day to see Angkor Watt temples which is why I came to Cambodia.

Below are pictures of charcoal rubbings I have from Angkor Watt which my mother-in-law had purchased when she and my father-in-law visited Cambodia in the 1950's.

    Bob and I boarded a motorcycle "rickshaw" and headed for Angkor Watt. The guard said no motorized vehicle could go onto the grounds. My driver waived my crutches at the guard, and he motioned us on through. First step accomplished.

I had studied on the computer and knew exactly where to look for these carvings on the temple walls. But, guess what, I couldn't even climb the first set of stairs. With my instructions, Bob wandered down these walls and found one of the rubbings.

It was not a waste of time for me because I did see lots of elephants in the park.

Strangler fig trees and creeping lichens are devouring the ruins. Angkor was the capital city of the Khmer Empire. The city and empire flourished from approximately the 9th to the 15th centuries.

　　Angkor Watt is truly amazing covering about 50 acres of temples with carved faces.

Vietnamese have strange appetites

We boarded the RV Amalotus and started our cruise down the Mekong River.

The Captain made sure my 91st birthday was special.

Ashore on sightseeing trips, Bob rode on bicycle tuk tuks. Can you imagine me on crutches getting on this thing!

No! I didn't have to do that. I took this picture of Bob as my taxi driver rode past him to our destination, a silk factory.

This is one of the silks made in this factory. Vietnamese styles are very beautiful.

The houses, being close to the river, are up on stilts. Many were raising chickens or rabbits under the house.

Some families live right on the river.

Below, a market on the river.

Every evening aboard we had entertainment.

And then we arrived in Saigon where the Mekong River empties into the Pacific. We stayed at a lovely hotel also honoring the elephant. The food was delicious.

There was a lovely pool on the roof with a bar and a swimming pool where we could look down on this big city.

This country has been great keeping track of me and setting up an appointment for a doctor to see my foot. It is comforting to know there is an SOS place most everywhere in the world where there are doctors to take care of any medical emergency. Poor Bob would have to sit and wait for me as I was taken to a separate place for x-rays.

The traffic is mostly motorcycles with at least two or more people riding on each one. The people are used to watching out for pedestrians, so you just venture out with great determination and pray, especially since many of the intersections are very large. We rode past the Russian and American Embassies. The next picture was taken out the window of our cab. There is a reflection on the window. Notice the people are wearing masks protecting against the fumes.

The map shows where all the SOS places are located in the world. A French lady doctor saw me first and then they took more x-rays. The next doctor was from South Africa.

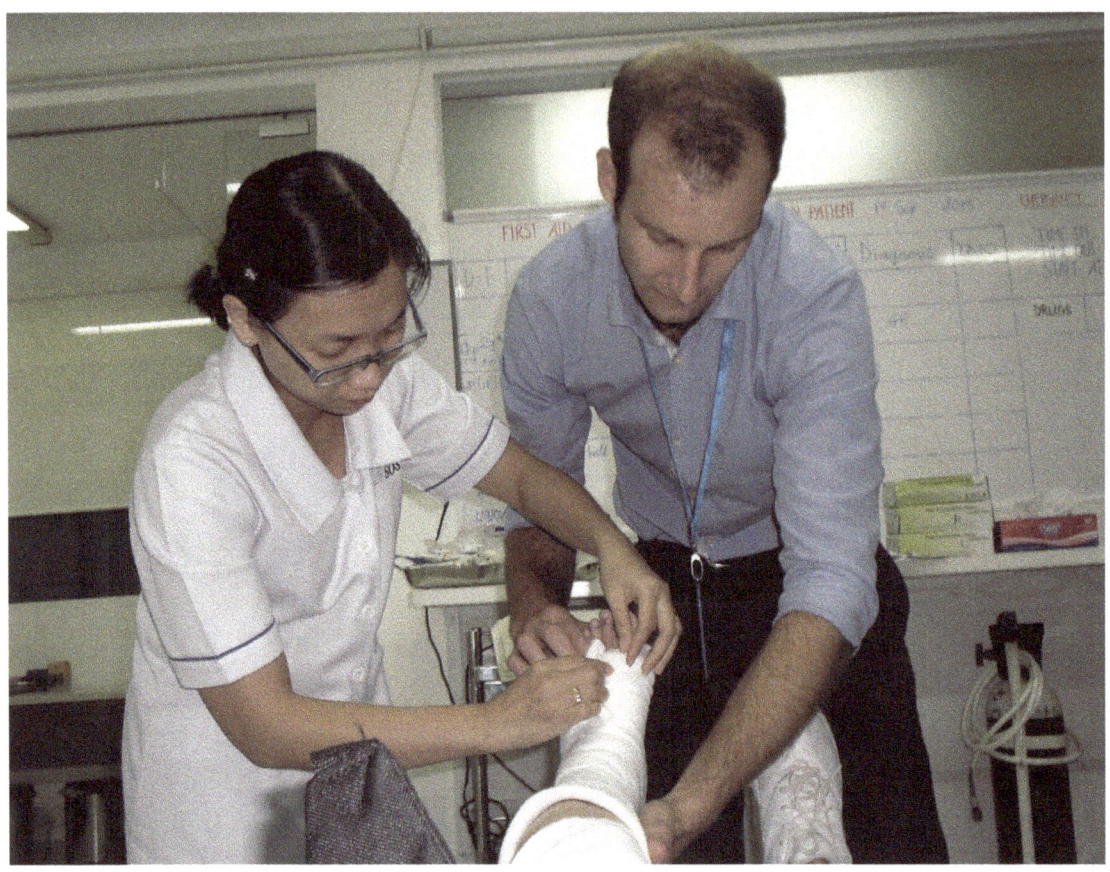

We could have taken a tour of the underground tunnels used by the Viet Cong during the Vietnam war, but there was no way I could crawl on my hands and knees. We were ready to head for home.

It did take several phone calls to our travel insurance people in New Hampshire to arrange for first class seats as my doctor issued an order that I must travel with my foot raised. Knowing we were on those crazy flights from Saigon to Seoul, Korea and on to Los Angles, I was thankful for a bed.

At the airport, a nice young girl pushed me around the airport, and we could see out the window our big two-story Korean Air plane awaiting us.

And more importantly, my bed!

This was my last trip with Bob as he passed away in 2017. I remember so well our last golf game. It was August just before my 93rd birthday. It was such a lovely warm, breezy day but not hot. I thought to myself, *If this is the last day, I ever play golf, it is a perfect day!*

As far as future planning goes, I still have a few destinations in mind, and they will no doubt be with one or more of my sons. Sadly, No. 2 son John and No. 5 son Tony have gone to heaven with their Dad. No parent should have the terrible pain of losing children. I thank the Lord every day I still have three sons, five granddaughters, one grandson, two great grandsons and two great granddaughters. Most importantly, Tony's wife, my daughter-in-law, Jessie, lives with me and takes great care of me.

Son Jim and I have had a competition going for many years to see who has visited the most countries. He was ahead of me until I went around the world and could say I had been on five of the six continents. Jim has not been to Africa.

Countries Visited

Far East	Europe	Caribbean	Central/So. America	Africa
Japan	Ireland	Jamaica	Mexico	Morocco
Korea	England	Grenada	Costa Rica	Egypt
China	Germany	Curacao	Panama	South Africa
Taiwan	France	Barbados	Columbia	Zimbabwe
Singapore	Austria	Dominican Republic	Brazil	Kenya
Thailand	Switzerland	Turks & Caicos	Argentina	Senegal
India	Italy	Cayman Islands	Uruguay	Uganda
Nepal	Greece	Aruba	Bolivia	Sudan
Malaysia	Spain	St. Thomas	Peru	
Cambodia	Jugoslavia	Bahamas	Ecuador	
Vietnam	Slovenia	St. Barts	Honduras	
	Croatia	Belize		
	Dalmatia	Cuba		
	Poland			
	Bosnia-Herzegovina		Canada	South Pacific
	Macedonia		Alberta	Tahiti
	Serbia		Quebec	Bali
	Montenegro		British Columbia	
	Netherlands		Ontario	
	Hungary			
	Czech Republic			
	Sweden			
	Denmark			
	Slovakia			

Key: Only Ginny; Only Jim; Jim/Ginny together; Jim/Ginny separately

Even though Jugoslavia is now broken up into many separate countries, I listed it because Jim and I visited it when it was still under Tito's thumb. Germany had lost the war and, as they retreated, they destroyed most of the roads. We saw a little cement mixer and three men working to repair a former main highway.

Tito was loosening his grip and allowing people to have a business with five employees. The only places we could eat were called buffets the poor people had opened in their own homes. We entered a home with only a meat counter with a couple pieces of sausage and an apple. The man sent his son down the street to get some bread to make us a sandwich. In one small town, we were driving the wrong way on a one-way street. The people came out to tell us of our mistake. It was hard to tell as we were the only car on the road.

Jim and I did visit the walled city of Dubrovnik. I was so impressed with the beauty and age as the red tiled roofs were covered with wildflowers blooming amongst the tiles. When Bob and I visited Dubrovnik on our Mediterranean cruise, I was so excited to show him these beautiful red tiled roofs covered with flowers growing in the dust of the ages. I was in shock when I found out that 80% of the roofs had been destroyed by bombing.

A nine-hundred-year-old bridge was also destroyed. My mom had her picture taken sitting on a bench the year before I visited for the first time. I had sat on the same bench. This was the war in 1999 between the Muslims and Christians which lasted three years and 100,000 people died.

I think I have now passed Jim on countries visited. My count: Jim, 62, me, 68. I'm waiting for his check on my chart.

When I asked Jac if he wanted to join us in this contest, he said, "Only if I can count the 30 plus times I have been to Japan.

Chapter Ten
Cuba and Family Reunion

For my 93rd birthday, Jim, Tom and Jac took me on a cruise from Miami to Cuba, stopping in Mexico and Honduras. It was during the brief few months that Cuba was open to Americans. Jim and I sailed out of Miami harbor and soon the sunset.

    I loved our 5 o'clock wine time aboard ship accompanied with a game of hearts. Much to their surprise, I beat them every day, thanks to my bridge acumen.

We did all the tourist things including riding around in a 1935 Chevy convertible in mint condition with a driver who loved to blow the horn.

My most recent trip was to California to attend the Nickoloff Family Reunion. My husband started the Nickoloff Family Reunions in 1984 at our home in Apple Valley, California. Jimmy had lost one of his favorite cousins and thought it a good idea to have a reunion before we lost anyone else.

They have continued over the years with the last one in Hollywood in 2019, celebrating the 100th wedding anniversary of my husband's parents, Jim and Mimi Nickoloff. We all had so much fun. The next one is being planned for Palm Springs in February 2021.

On my 96th birthday, my son Jim contacted all my nieces and nephews and we had a zoom meeting. My nieces told me how much they loved my Christmas gifts to them when they were little girls. I told them it was my pleasure since I didn't get to buy girlie things with only sons.

The Nickoloff family in Hollywood. My sister-in-law Betty and I (in the middle) were the matriarchs.

For the 1984 Reunion, I had made an apple family tree. I asked each person to send me a small picture that I attached to a branch, an apple or a blossom.

Below, the whole Apple Valley group with Grandpa Jim left of center in 1984.

These reunions happened every four years, sometimes in Northern California and sometimes in Southern California and one year in Hawaii at the ranch of my husband's sister, Nada, on the Big Island. Now we are doing every two years!

So, you see, planning ahead in my Platinum Years is not slowing down. In fact, I still have not seen the Florida Keys, easily accessible as Jim lives in Miami Beach. My granddaughter, Mary, and her husband picked the Keys for their honeymoon because she knew I hadn't been there! Sailing the St. Lawrence River is still on my agenda and Guanajuato, Mexico, keeps beckoning. Sailing the Mississippi River on a paddle wheeler would be great fun with all my little great grandchildren and their parents, of course.

Just remember one thing: if you don't plan, it won't happen!

Chapter Eleven
Exercise and Diet

Exercise is a most important component of making it through the Platinum Years. Bob and I put in our time at the gym (a year to be exact) before traveling to Africa. Time well spent! However, even more important is exercising every day. Granted, at 96, my walk over the dam or down to the three-way stop has been shortened to a walk up my driveway to get the mail and back. No "walker" yet, but I won't hesitate to use one when I feel the need.

To feel more secure walking up hill (to the mailbox), I lean forward. Walking back downhill, I tell myself "Baby steps and stand up straight."

Exercising is easy if it is a habit done every day. I have always started my exercise in the morning before I get out of bed. I lay on my back and pull one leg and then the other leg to my chest and then both legs together eight times. With knees on my chest, I turn them to one side and then the other side eight times. The eighth time, it throws me to a sitting position and with my arms outstretched, I twirl my hands eight times each direction.

It is always very important to sit on the edge of the bed before getting up. Sleeping all night, blood has been flowing horizontally. Now suddenly, it is flowing vertically. Beware, getting up suddenly can make an older person fall.

If you have leg cramps (as I do occasionally), put a tablespoon of apple cider vinegar in a glass of water and drink it each day until the cramps subside. Luckily, I haven't had cramps in a long time—could it be because I have been eating pickles? Who knows?

Standing, I swing my arms in circles eight times forward then backward. Next, I reach for the sky and then my toes. (I must admit I can't reach my toes anymore.) With arms at my sides, I lean to my right and then to my left, bending my body, reaching for my knees. Everything is done eight times, so I won't repeat that.

Exercising the neck is very important. First, I lean my head back and then forward eight times. Then side to side and then in a circle going left and then right. This must be done very slowly as sometimes you can hear creaking in your neck.

Bob was complaining about his neck hurting and I told him to do these exercises. Of course, he paid no attention to me and finally went to the doctor. When he came out, I asked him what did the doctor say? "He said to do the exercises you told me."

This next exercise I dreamed up myself. Remembering the old saying: "If you don't use it, you lose it." So, I applied this adage to my eye muscles, and I look up and down eight times. Then look left and right eight times. Then circle my eyes to the left and then circle to the right eight times. You can laugh all you want, but I use only glasses I get at the Dollar Store for reading and I can see across my lake to the marina and see cars going by on the road beyond the marina without glasses. And I don't use glasses to work on the computer.

The last exercise, I shake my hands, open and shut them, then spread each finger separately. I wish I had a brain exercise, but maybe writing this book will be exercising some of my brain cells.

Another idiosyncrasy I have is my day is regulated like clockwork, sort of like blocks of time. My radio alarm goes off at 8 a.m. and I listen to the news and then start my exercises in bed. Prepare coffee and my cereal. Take my pills and read my prayer books and the newspaper while I eat. At 12 noon, I eat my lunch, often an avocado sandwich with lemon-pepper. I don't think I need to tell you to go easy on the salt. I enjoy grapes or an apple or melon or mango and sneak a cookie.

Naptime is next for an hour unless I forget to set my mind. In that event, it could be several hours. Walk to the mailbox and read until 5 o'clock wine time and a phone conversation with one of my sons. Six o'clock, dinner time with Judy on PBS. This is followed by a Braves or Hawks game, or movie or reading a book until bedtime around midnight.

Exercise is good, but I think diet is even more important. You are what you eat. Remember that your stomach is the size of your two fists put together. Don't eat any more than that!

Cooking for my family of seven, six with huge appetites, they always answered, "hamburgers" when asked what they wanted for dinner. As a result, I stopped eating hamburgers myself and still never eat hamburgers. Luckily, McDonalds started making salads.

Habits can be good or bad. Hopefully, we all have more good than bad. My son Jim always complained I have a bad habit of hissing through my teeth and it drives him crazy. Actually, I have a song in my head, and I am humming it to myself. I can't help if he listens! What reminded me of this is, this morning I was "hissing" at the breakfast table and realized the song in my head was "It's 3 o'clock in the morning. We danced the whole night through!" You probably never heard that song and I can't believe it was still in my head. We had an old wind-up phonograph at our cabin and that was one of the records. I'm talking, the 1930's. Why would this song pop into my head 90 years later at the breakfast table? I guess our brains hold files bigger than a computer or anything we can comprehend.

Just remember: If you don't use it, you lose it!

Chapter Twelve
Pets and Plants

I sincerely believe that pets are good for the soul and certainly good company in the Platinum Years. There has never been a time when there wasn't a pet in our house. Certainly, no time without a cat.

At this time of my life, I enjoy two cats: Mooney and Sheba. Mooney is orange and born in the woods next door. Rescued by my son Tony, Mooney is still afraid of his own shadow. Sheba is pure white, smaller but she is certainly the boss. They have always slept with their "arms" around each other and they wash each other's face. If you have never had a cat, you probably don't know that they always "wash up" after they eat by licking themselves all over. In the winter months, one or the other or sometimes both cats are in my lap, enjoying the warmth.

When we picked up little Sheba from my granddaughter's neighbor, we were told that she loved pizza. She also enjoys corn on the cob!

As an only child, I was desperate for companionship. This is probably why I had five sons. They were born in the baby boomer years and were never lacking for companionship as there were 95 children on our very long block in Sierra Madre, California.

When I was a little kid in Long Beach, our neighbor would fish off the pier. One day, he brought me a cat that had existed on fish shared by the fishermen. The cat's name was Pete. If I really wanted Pete to come in a hurry, I just shouted "Fish, Pete" and he would come running. One day "Pete" had five kittens. About the same time, there was a cartoon in Reader's Digest of a society dowager with hands on her hips, looking down at a cat with kittens and saying: "Why, Pete?"

Another cat named Wooley Bear, I had from the time I was ten until after I was married and living in the little house behind my folks. Jimmy was going to law school and worked late at his Dad's restaurant. He was driving home about midnight when he ran over Wooley Bear sleeping in the driveway. Mom and I cried our eyes out and Jimmy said, "Well, she was old." And I said, "You wouldn't run over your grandmother just because she was old!"

My folks let me have any pet I wanted, and I had many. Besides cats and dogs, I had a horny toad, rabbits, Oscar the duck and Ignatz, a chameleon. Our No. 2 son, Jon, was the most into pets beginning when he was four years old and I found a hand full of worms in his pocket. Thank goodness I had learned to check all pockets before washing as Jon also collected snakes, seeds and plant cuttings and other strange things in his pockets.

Besides a huge aquarium, Jon had a parakeet named Jose and some temple birds.

The absolute worst pet was Mickey, Jon's monkey. Escaping his cage, Mickey was worse than a little kid as he could climb and open high cupboard doors. One day, he took a peanut butter jar into one of the boy's rooms and got peanut butter all over the shag carpet, impossible to remove. Remember shag carpets? Well, I replaced it with practical black and gray outdoor carpeting. Except for Jon, we were all happy when Mickey escaped and never came back!

Jon was always one with nature and brought home lizards from Grandpa's vacation house in Palm Springs. Over the years, I think we over-populated Sierra Madre with these lizards. Grandma Mimi was not happy when she found a rattlesnake in her freezer in Palm Springs. And one day I found a note on my refrigerator door saying: "There is a snake in the freezer. Don't eat it."

Another one of Jon's pets was a kangaroo rat. It was very large and fat. I hated that thing. One day, everyone had left for school and that damn thing (I don't usually swear) got out of its cage and ran behind the refrigerator. When it came out, our cat killed it with one bite on its neck. No regrets on my part.

Early one morning, I was standing at the kitchen sink (where I was most of the time) when I felt a small snake crawl over my foot. Jon's snake had nine babies and he had left their cage open accidentally. He was leaving for school and I ordered him to find every snake before he left. He did miss one that I later vacuumed up with no remorse.

Jon could make noises that would attract wild birds to his hand. He graduated with a degree in botany and spent months living in the Amazon jungles gathering fern spores. That adventure and his adventure attempting to live in the everglades like a caveman when he was 16 years old are stories told in *Grossly Outnumbered.*

One Sunday, when Tony was too young to go to away camp, Jimmy and I took him to Camp Bluff Lake in the San Bernardino mountains to visit his older brothers. At that time, Jon (17), was in charge of the camp's activities. Tony filled a cottage cheese carton with tiny tree frogs. The lid came off as we were driving home on the freeway and the little buggers were hopping all over the car. A good thing I wasn't driving!

Tony brought home a puppy that grew to be a big malamute. He trained Sheba to stand on her hind legs and to play dead. She lived a long life and moved with us from house to house. She and our cat King Farouk were best buddies.

Tony also had a guinea pig a lady at the market had given him, probably because it was pregnant. It soon had five babies. Jac had a white rat who chewed up his pillowcase.

We had a pregnant cat and I told my kids cats usually have five kittens so we would name each kitten after one of the five brothers. That one time, the cat had only three kittens: Jim, Jon and Tom. Sadly, I accidentally ran over Tom, the kitten, and son Tom has never forgiven me.

Jimmy's folks never allowed their family to have pets, but his mother got a parakeet in her old age. Mimi loved martinis, and her parakeet would sit on her glass and sip the martini. It would have a wobbly fly back to its cage.

My husband brought home a kitten from the dump in Carrollton, Georgia. He named him Catfish and would take him for rides on our pontoon boat. This is my favorite picture of Jimmy.

One wouldn't call flowers and trees pets, but I do have a certain affinity for growing things. I talk to my azaleas and address the dogwood trees as my little puppy dogs. The Chinese magnolia is named for my friend Maggie and the gingko tree is Gordy after an old friend in California. My camelia outside the office window is named for my granddaughter Camila.

Soon after Jimmy passed away, a lady came by with her son and a baby magnolia tree in a pot. She told me when Jimmy was on the Fairfield Board of Directors, he was very kind to her, and she wanted to bring this Chinese Magnolia tree as a memorial to him. Her son would plant it anywhere I chose. It has grown into this magnificent specimen I named Maggie after my good friend, Maggie Sullivan.

When Jimmy and I planted Gordy, he was about three feet tall and his purpose was to hide a telephone pole. However, he didn't grow at all. So annoyed with him, one day I bawled him out and told him he was out of here if he didn't straighten up and fly right! That did it! He has been growing rapidly ever since and is doing his job masking the telephone pole.

There was another purpose as in the Orient, gingkoes are planted near the front door to bring money into the house. It is called the money tree. I always greet Maggie and Gordy when I go to the mailbox.

Jimmy transplanted a dogwood from the backyard to the front yard twenty-five years ago. It grew but never flowered until this year. What a joy when spring arrives, and Georgia's blooms are busting out all over. Before we moved to Georgia, son Tom would call and tell me how beautiful the dogwood trees are in the spring. When we would come back to visit, he would say: "Too bad, Mom, you just missed the dogwood blooming." Now, a resident of Georgia, I enjoy the spring's flowering bonanza every year. My friend, Maggie, has always said that even shacks in Georgia are beautiful in the spring when azaleas and dogwoods are blooming in the front yards.

Speaking of Maggie, she was from Kansas where she told me if you make four right turns, you will end up in the same place. On the other hand, in Georgia, with four right turns, you could easily end up in another state.

To further confuse, streets can have several names. Son Jim advised me not to pay attention to street names in Georgia, just go by number. Highway 98 goes in all directions and covers most of Georgia and solves the problem when you can't get there from here.

One day, Bob and I were coming home from Kennesaw. We missed a turn and traveled for miles in unfamiliar territory. Since it was Sunday afternoon and a pleasant day, we saw a lot of Georgia we hadn't seen before. Miraculously, we had gone in a complete circle and ended up at the corner where we missed the turn. They say going in circles also happens when you are lost in the woods.

I still have a problem calling a freeway an interstate. Growing up with freeways in California did not prepare me for Georgia's interstates. Disliking the whole concept, I search out back roads and have even driven from Villa Rica to Miami on Highway 27 instead of Interstate 85. Highway 27 is a four-lane divided highway and very few trucks use it. For that matter, I also used Highway 27 to travel to Chattanooga and states north.

Of course, I did give up driving when I turned 90. Not because I had to, but because I never liked driving anyway and thought it best when one day, I hit a curb going around a corner. I even prefer riding in the backseat, so I deem myself the backseat rider, not driver. Another good thing about the backseat is that it makes a good place for sleeping! You know ... the thing I do best!

My mom was still driving at 92 and the state of Georgia mailed her a 10-year renewal of her license!

Chapter Thirteen
Jessie and Tony

The pandemic of 2020 is a worrisome thing, even more worrisome than polio was in the 1950's. Wearing a mask doesn't seem to be a problem so why don't people do it? They say old people like me are very likely to die if we catch the virus. I do miss my bridge and I really miss meetings with the Carrollton Writers Guild and my book club, but otherwise, staying indoors hasn't been a problem and, thankfully, I am not alone. When Tony and his wife Jessica moved in with me in 2008, it was so nice having a man in the house again.

But the best thing was they both loved to cook … not my favorite thing! I think the two of them planned dinner before they even got out of bed in the morning. "What spices shall we put on the lasagna?"

There are so many things that are hard for women to do as we found out when Tony passed away in 2018. I am ashamed to say I have a little list of things for Tom to do when he comes on Sunday.

Jessica came to the United States from Hong Kong with a girlfriend who planned on marrying a young man here in Georgia. The friend changed her mind and went back to Hong Kong. Jessie chose to stay here. Soon she met Tony and they fell in love at the beginning of this century. They were married in Marietta and soon after we celebrated their wedding at our house with the whole family.

Jessie studied hard and before long, Bob and I had the privilege of attending the ceremony celebrating Jessie becoming an American Citizen. It was thrilling watching all these people from all over the world dedicating themselves to being good citizens and "defending the United States against any foe." Each one was given an American flag.

Three days after she became a citizen, she received notice to serve on a jury. I have lived here thirty years and have never been called!

Jessie studied and became a licensed care giver. She now works three days a week in a nursing home, so I have the pleasure of her company four days a week. We supported each other during the dreadful days of Tony's terminal illness.

Lucky me, Jessie enjoys cooking. On days when Jessie works, she prepares my lunch and dinner ready in the refrigerator. I told you she is my angel guardian.

I cooked for my family of seven for 25 years. One day, I came home from playing golf and was taking one of my 30-minute naps on the couch. Jimmy came in and asked what are we having for dinner? My answer was "I don't have a clue." With that, he made a proposition I couldn't refuse. He would prepare dinner if I totally stayed out of the kitchen and offered no advice. I never did and he cooked. I ate whatever he cooked for the next 25 years.

Jimmy always loved to shop markets as well as hardware stores, and I preferred shopping department stores for clothes. At any rate, I promised not to recommend or suggest anything. His style was to just start putting stuff into a pot. A broad description would be he usually cooked a "stew." It could be anything such as a grapefruit cut up with skin and all mixed with some meat and vegetables. One I particularly remember was eating a pear when I thought it was a potato.

I do give Jimmy a disservice as he was very good at barbecuing owing to his father's owning the best barbecue restaurant in the city of Los Angeles. Grandpa Jim opened the Original Barbecue in 1936 and served the best barbecued chicken and ribs roasted on a rotisserie for the next 50 years. Besides grilling New York steaks, Jimmy added grilled catfish to his Georgia menu.

From the time of Jimmy's death until 2008 when son Tony and wife, Jessie, moved in, those eight years I ate out a lot and was pretty good at fixing leftovers from doggie bags.

That reminds me of the time we were celebrating Jimmy's brother Tom's 17th birthday at Lowry's restaurant on the famous "Restaurant Row" in Hollywood. You may be familiar with Lowry's seasonings available at all supermarkets (I'm never without Lowry's lemon-pepper.) Prime rib was Lowry's specialty served with the bone.

Remember this was before doggie bags. Making up an excuse for taking home the meaty bone from her serving, my mother-in-law Mimi told the waitress that she had a dog so would she bag it up for her. When the waitress came back, we cracked up when she gave Mimi a whole bag of bones from the kitchen for the non-existent dog! Perhaps that was the beginning of the doggie bag!

Chapter Fourteen
Poetry

After discussing the importance of planning and having pets in the Platinum Years, let me suggest another "p": poetry. Only recently have I spent a lot of time reading poetry, probably because I am pretty much housebound until someone finds a vaccine for corona virus. Some poems are funny, and some can touch your very soul.

My mom introduced me to poetry as a little kid with Mother Goose rhymes published in England in 1870 and Grimm's fairy tales. Some of these rhymes date back to the 1600's.

If you don't remember:

>This little piggy went to market
>This little piggy stayed home
>This little piggy had roast beef
>This little piggy had none,
>And this little piggy cried
>Wee, wee, wee all the way home.

you haven't held a baby in your arms.

Probably the first rhyme I learned was Star light, star bright, first star I see tonight. And who didn't play Ring Around the Rosie and all fall down! Three Blind Mice was written in 1609 and Jack Sprat could eat no fat, his wife could eat no lean, so betwixt the two, they licked the platter clean! (1639).

Who didn't play London Bridge is Falling Down and doesn't remember all the rhymes that accompanied playing jump rope and hopscotch?

Remember the seven-verse poem The Spider and the Fly written by Mary Howitt (1799-1888) begins with:

>"Will you walk into my parlor?" Said the spider to the fly;
>"T'is the prettiest little parlor that ever you did spy.
>The way into my parlor is up a winding stair.
>And I have many pretty things to show when you are there."
>"O no, no," said the little fly, "to ask me is in vain,
>For who goes up your winding stair can ne'er come down again."

And the last verse:

> And now, dear little children, who may this story read,
> To idle, silly, flattering words, I pray you ne'er give heed;
> Unto an evil counselor close heart, and ear, and eye,
> And take a lesson from this tale of the Spider and the Fly.

And what about:

> Little Miss Muffit
> Sat on a tuffit
> Eating her curds and whey
> Along came a spider
> And sat down beside her
> And she began to cry

This poem popped into mind when I was reading an article in the paper about making cheese and the cheese maker was pictured, stirring the curds and whey! I still don't know what a tuffit is?

Another favorite poem of mine is about two toys written by Eugene Field (1850-1895):

The Duel

> The gingham dog and the calico cat
> Side by side on the table sat;
> T'was half-past twelve, and, (what do you think!)
> Nor one nor t'other had slept a wink!
> The old Dutch clock and the Chinese plate
> Appeared to know as sure as fate
> There was going to be a terrible spat
>
> *(I wasn't there, I simply state*
> *What was told to me by the Chinese plate!)*
>
> The gingham dog went "bow-wow-wow!"
> And the calico cat replied "mee-ow!"
> The air was littered, an hour or so,
> With bits of gingham and calico,
> While the old Dutch clock in the chimney-place
> Up with its hands before its face,
> For it always dreaded a family row!
>
> *(Never mind: I'm only telling you*
> *What the old Dutch clock declares is true!)*

The Chinese plate looked very blue,
And wailed, "Oh dear! What shall we do!"
But the gingham dog and the calico cat
Wallowed this way and tumbled that,
Employing every tooth and claw
In the awfullest way you ever saw—
And, oh! How the gingham and calico flew!

Don't fancy I exaggerate—
I got my news from the Chinese plate!)

Next morning where the two had sat
They found no trace of dog or cat;
And some folk think unto this day
That burglars stole that pair away!
But the truth about the cat and pup
Is this: they ate each other up!
Now what do you really think of that!

(The old Dutch clock it told me so,
And that is how I came to know.)

Remember?

Beans, beans, musical fruit.
The more you eat, the more you toot!

In my mother's youth, students had to memorize poems or parts from Shakespeare. She could recite to me the six verses of "The Barefoot Boy" by John Greenleaf Whittier. She really had a much better education than I did in her little town in South Dakota. My elementary school curriculum was called "Progressive Education" and we really learned very little. The only thing that saved me was my ninth-grade teacher who taught us how to diagram a sentence.

Asking my mother the meaning or spelling of a word led to "Go look in the dictionary!" Nowadays, just go to Google or ask your cell phone or Alexa. Son Jac's daughter who is named Alexa does present a problem in their household.

My mother lived to 97 so part of my longevity is from her good genes. She was a voracious reader and reading came before TV. Jeopardy was one of the few programs she watched. She loved to sew, and I still treasure my wedding gown she created from my drawing of a wedding gown I saw in the May Company window.

Jac's daughter, Brielle, tried on my wedding gown and Jac put on his dad's Naval uniform for this photo op.

Mom not only created my wedding gown, but she also made all the bridesmaids' dresses, the flower girl' dress and her own gown for the wedding along with my beautiful trousseau. That was one reason our engagement lasted from one February to the next February to allow her time to create these beautiful dresses.

My mom used to sew for the neighbors to make a little spending money. One of our neighbors was Mrs. Peach who was very heavy, so Mom made a lot of her clothes. At this time, Kathryn Hepburn had started wearing "slacks" and Mrs. Peach wanted a pair of slacks! Mom obliged and they were so huge that my girlfriend and I each got into a leg and Mom took a picture of us. Of course, this was never seen by Mrs. Peach. And now I am ashamed of myself.

Another fashion note: the length of skirts in the thirties and forties changed every year and the movies played into this scheme to make your wardrobe outdated every year! My mother made me a gorgeous trousseau, all dresses stopping just above the knee. In fact, the skirt I wore with Jimmy to get our wedding license was so short and tight, Jimmy had to lift me into the car (a jeep). My mother covered the whole top of one of my dresses with handsewn sequins.

A year later, my friends gave me a baby shower and my cousin Jean, a student at Berkeley at the time, attended wearing a skirt to her ankles. We were all a little shocked, but, of course, she was right in style and all my beautiful trousseau was out of date one year later. Even worse was the fact I got pregnant and Jim was born one year and three days after we were married. I really didn't get to enjoy wearing mother's handiwork. She did make me some beautiful maternity dresses. Thank goodness, today, anything goes!

As happens in the Platinum Years, I got off the subject matter which is poetry. My mom wrote some beautiful poems and on target is the following poem:

The Lines Upon My Face

As the days go on and the years keep pace,
The wrinkles grew upon my face.
Around the eyes the first ones came.
Some say that smiling is to blame.
Then came the ones on cheek and chin
The cause of these? Perhaps a grin.
Who would a smooth face care to see,
That shows no sorrow, joy or glee?

I think the first small wrinkle was made
When I first looked at my wee babe.
For happiness etched the first one there
As I saw the answer to my prayer.
What joy, what hope, if I could know
That well and happy she would grow.
And so was furrowed upon my brow
Perhaps the wrinkle that I see now.

And as we have lived and loved together
The lines appeared upon the mother.
Some were for love and some for worry
As time moved on in such a hurry.
And when I reach my last deep sleep
Only upon my face I'll keep
The lines that through my life have grown,
Small bits of sorrow, great joys I've known.

My mom's poems bring tears to my eyes. She always seemed so stoic and could handle any challenge, I had no idea of her inner feelings. I always described my mother as someone who could have traveled across the country in a covered wagon with ten kids and had no problems doing it. She only had me, and I wasn't a challenge to her capabilities.

In the following poem, you can almost get into my mother's head:

My Tapestry

As I sit down and take into my hands
Some piece of needlework to weave a pattern thru,
I let my fancy travel into foreign lands
And I become a wanderer like you.
And when into its place a stitch I take
I wander in some foreign land bazaar,
And see some lovely tapestry I'd like to make
To hang upon my castle walls, afar.

Each color fits into its place, and then
I see a strange design begin to grow,
It does not seem to be of earth or men
But of a lovely land I do now know.

And as my threads of wondrous shade and hue
Fall into place and make a path of stone,
An old brick wall appeared, the flowers grew
To make my garden where I dream alone.

But 'ere my thread is gone, my work is done,
My pattern seems to change once more.
My garden wall and all its flowers are gone
And I am just the dreamer as before.

In this poem, I see my Mom's desire to travel. She was always checking out travel books from the library. However, my Dad had no interest to travel anywhere. The only vacation we ever took was to see Yosemite Valley when I was ten years old. That may be one of the reasons she divorced my Dad after twenty-five years of marriage. She had another twenty-five years of marriage with Les Cross and they traveled the world together.

When Les passed away, my Mom up and moved from California to Georgia when she heard that we "might" move to Georgia. She bought a big house with lots of bedrooms as she loved to have everyone come to "visit". By this time, she was 90 years old and she called me up one day and said: "I think I'll go to Arabia for Christmas." I couldn't have been more stunned. In fact, I thought she was losing her mind.

Not so! Her youngest sister's son was teaching English in Arabia and had invited her to come for a visit. She, a planner like me, flew from Atlanta to Chicago to Amsterdam for an overnight sleep and then on to Arabia, arriving at midnight. Her nephew was late picking her up at the airport, but she said, "I wasn't worried as all the sheiks were shorter than I am." That is hard to believe as she was only five feet tall. However, she wasn't afraid of anything or anyone; always strong as an ox and kept a billy club hanging on her bed post and a rifle under her bed. She knew how to use that rifle as she had gone hunting with her Dad in South Dakota.

Mom passed away in 2000, soon after my husband passed away. Her last poem:

A Grandmother's Ode to her Grandsons

My candlelight is growing dim,
as many years have passed for me
I drank the joys from the cups rim,
and gloried in every growing tree.

The flowers gave forth their glorious bloom,
and every weed blessed our God, too.
Then began a time of wars and gloom
and all the world was sad and blue.

We grew a little more each year,
and walked some more upon life's road.
And gathered friends from far and near,
who helped us carry our great load.

And then the family unit grew,
you five dear boys who came to me,
have made my life itself renew
and then this poem made life come true!

My cousin Jean, the artist, and I were only 13 months apart. I lost her a couple months ago and would like to add one of her poems that is very apropos. The punctuation is hers.

BEFORE I DIE

Before I die, I want to do a hundred things
a hundred things to do before I die

Before I die, I want to watch the sunrise
over the Taj Mahal and marvel at love

Before I die, I want to have a wild affair
On a train, with a tall dark stranger

and not just any train, the Orient Express
passing through Budapest before I am stiff

Before I die, I want to drink slivovitz and eat a
hard roll for breakfast on a wall in Dubrovnik

Or have a perfect meal at a truly great French
Restaurant prepared just for me, such joy

Before I die, I want to ride a wild horse
Across the grasslands with the tartars

Before I die, I want to spend Christmas
at the Ahwahnee, martini in hand near half dome.

Before my time is up, I want to climb
the Eiffel tower, the pyramid, K2

and raft the middle fork of the salmon river
before the earth settles over my face

Before I die, I want to spend a weekend
at the only alpine meadow in the U.S.A.

Before I die, I want to do a hundred things
maybe ten or twelve, or if I'm lucky, --one!
                      Jean Clad

    She was a very special and talented person. She lost the sight of her right eye at the age of five. It never stopped her from doing anything and I know she did raft on the Salmon River with her son, Chris and my son, Tony. She also climbed Mount San Jacinto with the two boys in the winter with snow on the ground.

    Jean met her husband, Noel Clad, at Berkeley and the two of them went to Paris so they could study at the Sorbonne. They were married by the Mayor of Paris. Noel had been a paratrooper during World War II and landed in the Italian Alps bringing food to our troops. He was hired after the war by someone in charge of the Marshall Plan that put Europe back on its feet. He and Jean lived in Trieste and she had an art show in Rome. The Italian newspaper described her style as American Primitive. Back in the United States, Noel pursued his writing career and published some novels.

Jean lost her husband in an airplane accident when their son, Chris, was two years old. She earned her living teaching painting at the college level and organized many art shows in Long Beach, California. Her art lives on in many homes in California and in my house and son Tom's here in Georgia, as well as a lovely Italian landscape loved by my son Jim in Miami. Her reference in her poem is to the Ahwahnee Hotel in Yosemite National Park. She loved to hike and enjoyed martinis.

Jim fell in love with this scene of Tuscany hanging in Jean's kitchen. She loved to paint the rolling hills of Tuscany. It is now hanging in Jim's place in Florida.

Another one of Jean's paintings of Tuscany that I love.

Next are some of Jean's paintings that hang in my daughter-in-law Dixie's house.

Because I could only copy, I admire Jean's flare for color that she used with total abandon!

I love Jean's happy face in this picture with Jac taken at a wedding. A true artist, she loved putting different colors on her hair.

     Again, I got off the subject of poetry. No.1 Son Jim sent a beautiful birthday card to me when he was living in Korea in 1971. It was a painting on rice paper of bamboo with the following poem he composed:

>Sitting on the hillside crowded
>>with green-growing-things.
>
> Looking across the valley and
>>the uncountable tiny
>>paddies tall with rice
>
>Slightly dizzy with full Summers'
>>heavy sweet breath
>
>Thinking of home—but really
>>of the people there.

No.3 Son Tom wrote a poem for Valentine's Day:

BUTTERFLY

How fine are those who float on air,
and fly so light with grace and care.
No sounds are heard as you go by,
You're hard to catch although I try.
You dance and dart and jump and flee
As if to say, "you can't catch me!"

The amazing colors on your wing,
reveal the magic that you bring.
The reds and golds, the shades on white,
Yes, all those colors in all their might.

I wonder how you came to be,
thank God and Son for you from me.
How great He is who brought you here,
for me to see it's all so clear.

As you go, I'll lose this sight,
But I'll never forget your colors bright.
Next time you start your day so free,
Please fly your wings back home to me.

Tom Nickoloff 2012

And No. 5 Son Tony wrote an interesting (strange) poem called:

CYCLONE

Incurious acts that defy
A hymn of wisdom collides.
Two lads see unrest,
And just beyond the fence.

Race with a cyclone,
On the horizon
A wild wind undressed,
And sure to the test!

A furious tide of life stealing art,
Riches to rags and miles apart,
The raiding wind and next of kin,

Reckoning scars and upside-down cars.

The gale it's past and all's at ease
A solemn breeze as nature's knees
No plate with forks,
No bottle with corks.

A maize of mesh, three deep abreast
A nail for a rest, a badge on a vest.
This sense of loss, will not last...
'Cause lucky for me, I saw it on TV!

I was moved to write a poem when we celebrated our 50th wedding anniversary. My brother-in-law, Tom and his wife, Betty and Jimmy and I flew to Acapulco, Mexico, to celebrate their 40th wedding anniversary and our 50th.

OUR GOLDEN ODYSSEY

It was our beginning – our honeymoon,
South of the Border, down Mexico Way.
Acapulco, then a tiny village
Nestled in one small curve of a crescent

Like the bay, we came near full circle
Returning fifty years hence
To discover a city of millions
Stretching its boundaries from tip to tip.

Our casita perched on the side of a cliff
Offered a private pool of floating hibiscus
And each evening the setting sun disappeared
Into a calm Pacific turning it from blue to red.

Our favorite time of all to be together,
To hold hands and remember our shared dreams
Was when the night turned the bay and the sky
To black velvet, like a jeweler's tray.

And the sparkling city lights became a tiara
Of glistening diamonds, emeralds and rubies
Surrounding us with a brilliant display
And drawing us together as one forever.

Enough of that mush!

My interest in anything Japanese or Chinese since childhood, led to my enjoyment of the Japanese haiku style poetry. One day, lying in my new jacuzzi sunken tub, looking at the bamboo fenced Japanese garden out the big window in Apple Valley, I composed the following haiku:

The Jacuzzi Tub

My body is still,
  Floating in the water.
Rushing over and under,
  Bubbles rise around my head.

My mind is drifting.
  Submerged in the sounds,
Pleasant and hypnotic.
  Dreams come easily.
Slowly reality returns.
  Stopping the waters churning,
My body is still again,
  Weightless, floating.

I listen to the bubbles
  Bursting quietly around me.

As the water gurgles and lowers,
  My body slowly rises.

Heavier and heavier
  My body becomes.
The last big shoosh
  And then………

Like a Phoenix
  My body unfolds.
Standing under a cool refreshing shower
  The Odyssey ends.

When I visited Japan to attend a wedding, we stayed at a Japanese Inn. I had read the book, *Japanese Inn*, by Oliver Statler, about the 400-year-old Minaguchiya Inn on the Tokaido Road built in 1603. This road joined Kyoto, residence of the Emperor to Edo (now Tokyo), seat of the executive government of the shoguns. Inns were spaced the distance a horse could ride in a day along this road. There were 53 stages and the Minaguchiya Inn was the 17th stage at Okitsu, only a few miles from Shimizu where the wedding would take place.

I was so excited I immediately wrote to the Minaguchiya Inn to make a reservation. This was before computers. Weeks went by and I didn't receive an answer. Finally, I called Yuki, the groom, and he made the reservations for us explaining that Japanese people think Americans wouldn't want to sleep on the floor.

The door of the Inn was right on the street and our shoes disappeared immediately on entering only to miraculously appear whenever we were ready to leave. Inside, miniature gardens kept unfolding as we were escorted to our suite overlooking Suruga Bay. It was all there! Tatami mats, sliding shoji walls and a tokonoma, an alcove displaying a beautiful flower arrangement. Our meals were served on a low table, our legs stretched out underneath. And the 8-inch-thick mattress on the floor was prepared each evening by little men so quiet, they were almost invisible.

At dawn the next morning, I set out on foot to walk through the tiny village of Okitsu. I was bound for the ancient temple Seikenji described in Statler's book. Seeing the bell tower, I climbed a little path beside the temple. I could hear tinkling bells in the Buddhist pattern: ding, ding … ding, ding, ding … followed by a heavy dong! I climbed to the top above the temple with the bell sounds repeating as the monks said their prayers inside the temple. I wondered if they knew I was there. I walked back to the inn lost in thought, composing my first haiku:

Morning Reflections

The mountain trail
  Climbs higher and higher.
Mountain spirits smile,
  A dream comes true.

The curving roofs
  reach toward the sky
The bell tower awaits
  A joyous sound.

Raindrops fall on
  The mossy path.
Silently one hundred
  Stone monks pray.

One stone monk weeps
  While ages pass
Like flocks of swallows
  Riding the wind.

The gray sky cries.
  A willow weeps.
Goodbye, Seikenji,
  I shall come back.

My pilgrimage
  Comes to an end.
Miniguchiya,
  You are Japan!

That was such an emotional experience for me that tears came when I finished reading it at my Writers' Guild meeting. Probably because I knew I wouldn't be back.

Apparently, poetry runs in our family, as my mom's first American born Grandfather, Samuel Doak, wrote these verses on the occasion of his marriage in October of 1775:

The hour is come, we join our hands,
  And bind ourselves in wedlock bands,

> In presence of Almighty God to vows perpetual,
>> There we read: "Tis past."
> Then first of all we pray
>> That God may bind our souls today
> In bonds of everlasting love;
>> Commenced below; improved above
>> Then whilst our moments wing heavenward
>> And bare us to heaven the final day
>> Oh, may each heart be true
>> In honor of our Savior God
>> Nor accustom our unhallowed lust
>> Nor glittering stores of worldly dust
>> Nor all the tempting arts of man
>> Could then our hearts cement in one.
>> Great God, our witness, 'twas thou than joined
>> Our hearts and hands, and formed our mind
>> For social intercourse; then may
>> Our Souls as one here—Join to pray.

This is an old one:

> Monday's child is fair of face
> Tuesday's child is full of grace
> Wednesday's child is full of woe
> Thursday's child has far to go
> Friday's child is loving and giving
> Saturday's child works hard for a living
> Sunday's child born on the Sabbath Day
> is bonny and bright and good and gay

I was a Monday's child born on August 25, 1924. Son Tom could never remember my birthday, so I told him to just think of Christmas in August. Get it? He didn't.

Anxiously, I have been waiting for word of the birth of my fourth great grandchild. Happily, the wait is over and little Clementine Simone McFall was born on Saturday, July 11, at 2 minutes to midnight. The date 7/11/20 will be easy to remember. Thank goodness for e-mail as who knows when I will see this baby.

My son Tom was born 2 minutes to midnight on March 16. My doctor told me it would be little Patricia born on St. Patrick's Day. He was wrong on both counts!

My granddaughter Lauren and husband Scott live in Ashville, North Carolina. The plan was for her dad Jac to fly to Georgia and take me to see the new baby. Corona virus ruined that plan. When, oh when, will I see this new bundle of joy?

The birth of Clementine moved my son Jim to write her a letter. Her mom Lauren replied that she has put the letter in Clementine's Baby Book for her to read when she is old enough.

14 July 2020

Dear Clementine,

I am writing this letter to your parents, but I am really writing to you--even though I know it will be years before you can read it.

Yesterday was your first full day "in the world." I was thinking about this as I sat on the beach at sunrise here in South Beach, as I do on many mornings. I have a routine that I call "The Three P's"--which refers to prayer, Pilates, and then a plunge into the ocean. It's a great way to start the day. During the time of "prayer," I hold in mind and heart the many people that I love, including your parents and you over the past few months. But yesterday was the first day that I had a mental picture of your face, and that made it special.

The world you have been born into has many serious problems, as you will find out soon enough. At the moment, we are living in the midst of a worldwide pandemic, making it impossible for Robert and me to visit you in person in the foreseeable future. But we also face the apparently intractable problems of environmental destruction, racism, war, and all kinds of injustices. It is my hope that you will be a person who helps our human family find a way to face and solve these problems--for the sake of your well-being and the well-being of all. Let me also say that many people in my generation--and your parents' generation too--have done our best. But we have not yet succeeded. It will fall to you and your cousins--Maxtone, Avery, Natalie, and others who may come along--to bring this work to completion.

I also hope that your life is blessed with a sense of deep human satisfaction. Despite all the problems today--and yesterday--and tomorrow--I can say that at 72 years old I have come to realize how important a sense of fulfillment is. I am deeply grateful for our family, for my friends, for the work I have been able to do, and for the places I have been able to live. Though Life can be painful, it is beautiful and meaningful. I hope and pray that you come to know Beauty, Meaning, and Fulfillment in abundance! Give your parents my love and thank them for bringing you to us. You are a ray of sunshine.

(signed) Great Uncle Jim

Jim wrote this in long hand which brings up a problem I have with modern times, the demise of longhand writing. Clementine will no doubt have to get someone to read it to her. How many remember making circles in penmanship? Dipping those wooden pens with inserted points into inkwells on your desk? Ball point pens did solve that problem, but there is something personal and special when a note is handwritten.

Another demise along that line is reading the time on an analog watch or clock as opposed to a digital watch or clock. I think this change came in England before the United States. So how are children going to read the time on Big Ben? Hang in there, Big Ben! Don't let them change your beautiful face!

As the mother of five boys, I have been the happy grandmother of five girls and one boy: Tom's daughters Mary and Camila and Jac's daughters Lauren, Brielle and Alexa and his son, Brad. I have two great grandsons, Brad's son, Maxtone and Granddaughter Mary's son, Avery and her daughter Natalie. Granddaughter Lauren's baby, Clementine will be a playmate for 2-year-old Great Grand-daughter, Natalie. Now that you are totally confused, just remember that my Platinum Years have been blessed with a big family. And at last, lots of girls!

Ginny   Brad   Mary   Alexa Brielle/Maxtone Camila   Lauren

This picture of me with my grandchildren was taken at Mary's wedding.

Brad, wife, Melissa and Maxtone live in California. Mary and Camila live in Georgia. Alexa lives in Colorado with Dad Jac. Brielle lives in Washington, D.C. and wherever her job takes her. Her job is with voice recognition like Alexa. Her sister, Alexa, has a problem in their house in Colorado, with machine Alexa answering every time anyone says Alexa.

Camila is in her last year of high school. Unfortunately, she must do her school work on the computer at home because of the virus. Please, Lord, let the virus be defeated so that she may have a normal graduation next year with a prom.

Below, are my great grandchildren, Mary and Aaron's two children, Avery and Natalie.

They remind me so much of Brad and Lauren when they were little. They were a little older than Avery and Natalie when I was making the bed and there was a piece of wrapped candy on the nightstand. Brad asked me if there was another piece. I said "no" and started to say, "so you had better eat it before Lauren comes." Brad put it down and said, "Then I won't eat it." He was a very protective brother of his sister, just like Avery. Lauren and Brad are now in their thirties. Here is a picture of my Mom, their Great Grandma, holding Brad and Lauren.

My other great grandson Maxtone lives in California with his Mom Melissa and Dad, Brad, my grandson. They come to visit me and enjoy my lake.

My Platinum years have also been blessed with meeting new friends. A neighbor, Stephanie Baldi, was writing a novel. As she was writing, she would forward each chapter to me by e-mail and I became a "beta reader," a term used to describe a test reader who gives feedback on an unpublished work from the perspective of the "average" reader. This book, *Redemption*, is very exciting and she not only got it published, but she was nominated for Georgia Author of the Year. She has since published a sequel *Retribution* and is working on the third book in the series.

Stephanie introduced me to the Carrollton Writers Guild which meets once a month at the Carrollton Center for the Arts. Members read and critique each other's writings. I am happy to be a member of this group and really miss seeing them during our corona lockdown. You can see and read about our members on CarrolltonWritersGuild.org website.

Dee Dee Murphy is one of the members who writes a column regularly in the Times-Georgian newspaper. Since this chapter is about poetry, here is one that Dee Dee wrote for the Fourth of July issue of the Times-Georgian:

Anthem 2020   Dee Dee Murphy 7/4/20 ©

"Oh, say can you see what this year's done to me"
I so proudly proclaim, but I can't take a knee

on the field. So I pray for a much better day
and every injustice will just melt away.

In the rocket's red glare all our faults are laid bare,
for the whole world to see, and to fix if we care.

It's finally time, the reckoning is here
and the change that we want for our country is near.

Everyone say their name: Floyd, Taylor, and McClain;
and march day and night so they died not in vain.

We protest and contest the reasons they died.
Let's face it, it's past time we all pick a side.

Other names on that list, they need to be spoke
much more is needed, we need be woke.

Confederate symbols? It's time that they fall
so our public space will be welcoming to all.

I do want to love our amber waves of grain
but meet me half-way — do you feel my pain?

We take small steps then big ones and hope that one day
we're treated equal before to rest we lay.

There's no reason not to, ye family of man
we will make it happen, you bet that we can.

> We'll face the rising sun of our new day begun
> and we'll march on 'til victory is won.
>
> whose broad stripes and bright stars are more than a flag
> that banner should unite us and then we can brag
>
> that the streets and the plains came together to make
> a more perfect union for our children's sake.
>
> O say let those protests make red, white and blue
> proud colors for everyone; for me and for you.

I am happy to report Carrollton had a 'Protest" gathering in the square after the murder of the black man in Minnesota by the policeman and everyone danced together including the policemen.

Another member of the Guild is Frank Allan Rogers whose wife, Mary, is a talented artist who designs his book covers and also has art shows of her own. Mary is my guardian angel on the computer. She has spent hours helping me put the pictures in this book. These two are very special friends and have been keeping me in books to read since the coronavirus-19 kept me housebound.

Stephanie also brought me a big stack of books to read and son Jac ordered a book for me from Amazon: *The Better Angels of Our Nature*: *Why Violence Has Declined*, (696 pages). I'm struggling with this one, and hope the premise is true.

My morning reading of the Bible have brought me to the Book of Micah. I'm almost finished with the Old Testament: Micah 4:3:

> Nation shall not lift up
> > Sword against nation
> > Neither shall they learn war anymore

Chapter Fifteen
Letters

After reading the last chapter, I hope you look at poetry in a little different way and maybe will write a poem of your own. Over my lifetime, I have collected letters from family and friends, and I worry and wonder if letter writing is a thing of the past. One is probably not going to save a cell phone message or an e-mail. Have letters gone the way of dial phones?

Since Jimmy and I fell in love eight hours after meeting on a blind date, we had only one night to get acquainted before he left for Corpus Christi by train to be taught to become a pilot in the Navy during World War II. His cousin, Art, was dating and, later, married my friend, Marlyn Fredrickson. Marlyn called me to see if I would go to a show with them and Art's cousin, Jimmy, who was on leave. We saw Mickey Rooney in "Double Trouble".

I knew Jimmy was leaving the next day on the train for Corpus Christi, Texas. When he took me home, I was disappointed he didn't ask me for my address, so I asked him if he wanted it. (Boy, was I brazen!) He wrote it down on something in his wallet. Years after we were married, I discovered he was still carrying it in his wallet.

That was May 21, 1944, and we always celebrated that date. In fact, one night, we were celebrating at the Apple Valley Inn and Jimmy told the waiter we were celebrating the 17th anniversary of the day we met. I think he thought we were nuts.

The next few years after our meeting, our connection was only via letters. I have a whole box full. Every anniversary we would take one out and read it. I just now reached in the box and pulled out one of the first letters Jimmy wrote to me. Surprisingly, he had quoted this:

> In bed we laugh, in bed we cry;
> And, born in bed, in bed we die.
> The near approach a bed may show
> Of human bliss to human woe.
>   Isaac DeBenserade (1612-1691)

The amazing truth is he did die in bed December 18, 1999.

Jimmy went from Corpus Christi to Florida where he trained to land his plane on a carrier. Then he was transferred to Indio, California, and I was hundreds of miles away working in Yosemite. Still only letters, and then he was sailing to Hawaii when the bomb was dropped on Japan. He stayed in Hawaii for a while before being discharged from the Navy. On his return home, he proposed, and the rest is history.

Jimmy proposed to me on this night at a Hollywood nightclub and we agreed to never fight with each other. And we didn't!

Unbelievably, I received the following letter dated March 10, 1990, from Jimmy's cousin Art's sister. Art was the cousin who died very young that prompted Jimmy to have family reunions.

Dear Ginny,

I've been wanting to get this to you since I first found it at my mom's house (years ago). Jim wrote it to Art after your first date, but unfortunately the first page of it has disappeared, so no date.

The letter head:

OTTUMWA,

NAVAL AIR STATION

"... has a plane and two cadets fly wing on him for an hour and a half—that's the length of the periods. That gives us a nice three plane formation. Most of the period is spent in a "V" formation. We usually fly two periods a day which is plenty.

Hey, chum, I want to thank you and Marlyn for the swell time on that date we had, but even more I want to thank you for "the date." Boy, that Ginny is quite a gal. Man alive, I fell madly in love with her the first time I saw her. I have written her twice and received one letter from her. It's her time to write now. Boy, what a gal!

Guess you noticed the letterhead on this paper. Hope you will excuse it. I bought so much at Ottumwa, Iowa. I haven't bought any down here (Corpus Christi) yet. Well, Art, guess I'll close now, and I'll probably be hearing from you soon, huh?

Your Cousin, Jim"

You can imagine how thrilled I was to receive this letter 40 years later and know that we both fell in love at the same time.

In January 1997, I saw an article in the paper with a London date line:

LONDON (AP) Her children's marriages didn't last, but hers did – and Queen Elizabeth II is inviting other long-married couples to a 50th anniversary bash. The Queen on Monday invited other couples married in 1947 to apply for the 4,000 invitations to her July 15 party in the palace gardens. Applications--accompanied by a marriage certificate—must be in by Feb. 14.

"Long marriages are a feature of all walks of life and the garden party will give the queen and the duke an opportunity to meet people from a wide range of life experiences," a palace spokeswoman said.

Realizing Jimmy and I shared the same 50 years of "wedded bliss", I wrote a letter to the Queen with the help of a British friend of mine, Mary Sarner. In fact, Mary lost her husband recently and moved back to England.

January 24, 1997
TO HER BRITANNIC MAJESTY
QUEEN ELIZABETH II
    Your Majesty:

An article pertaining to Your Majesty's celebration of Your 50th Wedding Anniversary appeared in our local newspaper, The Times-Georgian. A Palace spokeswoman said, "Long marriages are a feature of all walks of life and the garden party will give the Queen and the Duke an opportunity to meet people from a wide range of life experiences."

On February 16, 1947, my husband James Nickoloff and I were married in Los Angeles, California. He was a Naval Air Force pilot in World War II and returned to college after we were married. Four sons later, he graduated from law school. Our fifth and last son was born in 1959.

We raised our boys in Sierra Madre, a small town in California where we resided almost thirty years. Sierra Madre is two miles long and one mile wide nestled in the foothills. Its charm must have captured the hearts of some British subjects because a British Home was established there in 1931 providing a residence for elderly persons of British Commonwealth birth or parentage and sponsored by the Daughters of the British Empire in the United States of America.

We often attended their annual June Fair and the fall "In-Gathering." A large portrait of Your Majesty hangs in the Salon. It was like a little bit of England in our midst. Eventually young British couples settled there also and introduced soccer to our small boys.

Several times over the years, the British Home has been honored by visits from Princess Margaret and Princess Alexandra and on one occasion, Prince Philip was in California for the Olympic Games in Los Angeles. His Royal

Highness was presented with "Victory's Gate," a bronze equestrian sculpture by Michael Wilson, a friend of one of our sons.

Our oldest son, James, now 48 years old, did a science fair project when he was fourteen years old which involved requesting an ounce of soil from each state in the United States and places all over the world, including Alice Springs, Australia; Durban, South Africa; and Swindon, England. A neighbor was surprised to receive a clipping from her family in Swindon which announced: "An ounce of Swindon goes to the U.S.A.!"

For the last six years, we have resided in a small suburb of Atlanta, Georgia. Amazingly, one of our neighbors of British descent is a member of the Atlanta Chapter of the Daughters of the British Empire. Each year she has invited me to their annual luncheon which is a fund raiser for the other British Home in Texas.

Perhaps Your Majesty would be interested to meet an American couple who shared those same fifty years of marriage. I am enclosing a copy of our marriage certificate. We would be honored to be considered for an invitation to Your Majesty's Celebration on July 15, 1997.

Jimmy promised, if we are invited, we will go!

We received an answer from Buckingham Palace dated March, 1997:

Dear Applicant,

I am commanded by The Queen to thank you for your recent letter, concerning the Garden Party to be given by The Queen and The Duke of Edinburgh on Tuesday, 15th July 1997, for couples who were married in 1947, as part of the celebration to mark the Golden Wedding of Her Majesty and His Royal Highness.

I regret to say you are ineligible to apply for this occasion as The Queen is not the Head of State of your country. Indeed, in view of the heavy demand, it will not be possible to invite every eligible couple wishing to attend as only a total of 4,000 couples can be invited.

However, Her Majesty was interested to learn of your anniversary and hopes that you will much enjoy your own celebrations.

I am sorry to send you this disappointing reply,

>Yours, sincerely,
>(an unreadable signature)
>State Invitations Assistant
>Lord Chamberlain's Office

In other words: You are not one of us.

Another missile received with the BUCKINGHAM PALACE letterhead:

The Lord Chamberlain presents his compliments and thanks you for the enclosed attachments in support of your application to attend the Golden Anniversary Garden Party, which are returned for your safe keeping.

Queen Elizabeth and I are both enjoying our Platinum Years. She is 95 and unfortunately lost Prince Philip in 2021. He was 99. Queen Elizabeth's mother died at 104. Alexa gave me all this information. (Easier than looking it up on Google.)

With the invention of cell phones, I predict that in another million years, we will consist of a head with one finger and no body. Maybe that is a little extreme, but something to think about.

I have always kept a file for each son with their letters and other memorabilia. If you live to your Platinum Years, your mind is full of memories. A little suggestion: When I am trying to think of something or someone, I just ask my mind to look around in my brain and come up with the answer. Sometimes it takes a while, but amazingly, it will eventually pop up.

I treasure letters from my boys and birthday cards and Valentines. When you become an empty nester, these missives become very important. Jim, the oldest, was the only son who left home at 17 and never lived at home again. Thankfully, he was the best letter writer and they came from all over as his travels took him to France, Russia, Korea, Jamaica, and Peru.

Jim (remember Jimmy is my husband, Jim, my son) spent a year as an exchange student, attending Stanford in France. At this point in his life, he had 8 years of Russian and 8 years of French under his belt. He and his fellow exchange students in Tours, France, took a train trip to Russia during their Christmas vacation.

The following letter came from Warsaw, Poland, dated December 21, 1968:

Snow everywhere. The air is like the coldest night air in California. All day. All night. A city of night. Dark at midmorning. Dark in mid-afternoon. At high noon there are low grey clouds which obscure all light. Dark grey buildings, warm pink people. Rows and rows of drab apartment houses, but big open spaces everywhere. Nowhere is there any green, or blue of the sky. Or yellow of the sun. Just white everywhere. But this is Warsaw.

"Ten minutes to the border."

"Just think, the Iron Curtain." The snowfall in Vienna had made the cold worth it. But Prague is ahead. Prague! Invaded city! What will we find?

"Look at the countryside. Just like a picture post card of New England. We will have a white Christmas."

"Dpabenibyume! (Hello) Are you in the Czech army?"

"Yes, I am."

"Would you mind speaking in Russian?"

"I would rather not."

But he wanted to communicate. As do all Czechs ……with all Americans.

In a beer hall about fifteen middle-age Czechs gather around a group of American students. "We in America do not understand why the Russians came."

"We in Prague do not understand why they stay." The conversation continued on into the night with the twenty-one-year-old Czech soldier.

Russian was better than silence. "What are you doing now in the way of lessening the Russian grip?" "Nothing can be done."

The sightseeing tours of Europe—very good, very interesting, but about the same. More monuments, more palaces, more kings, more people in each European capitol, too, but here they are different. There is only one thing on their minds, one thing only: Freedom. Freedom from Russia. They do not hide their constant thought. On a building: "Viva Dubcek". On a bus window written in the frost "Russians go home". A young Czech said, "The greatest sight I ever saw was a Russian tank burning the first day of the invasion. "What can be done?" The same answer: "Nothing!" There are soldiers everywhere, military trucks everywhere. Prague is a military base. Looks just like a World War II movie.

Warsaw was destroyed 85%. And 50 % of its population destroyed. Mostly after German defeat was certain. But destroyed by retreating Germans. Of course, it is today a modern city. Virtually everything has been built in my lifetime. Still, it remains plain. When you have no money for food, you do not waste it on beautiful architecture. "Communism was the only answer for Poland's economic recovery. We did not have American money as did Germany and Japan to start the investments rolling."

Jim was twelve years old in 1960 when dictator Khrushev banged his shoe on the desk at a United Nations meeting. This was the height of the Cold War and Jim was watching this happen on TV. He came out into the kitchen and said to me: "I want to know what he said and not what they said he said." Russian was available at Pasadena High School, so Jim started studying there and continued Russian at Stanford along with French.

The students were told not to bring any books as they would be taken away from them. One girl hid a book under her clothes on her back and she was sent into a room to undress. The rest of the students went on across the border and thankfully, she did join them soon but without her book.

This was just a short time for Jim to practice his Russian. He had another opportunity when the summer after his graduation from Stanford, Jim received a scholarship from Kansas University to attend Leningrad University for one whole summer. This was during the Cold War and competition between Russia and United States was high. That summer the first of the nineteen USA-USSR Track and Field Dual Games was being held at Leningrad University.

Jim and his fellow students tried to get tickets to the games that were within walking distance of their dorm. The "authorities" insisted there were no empty seats so forget it! Not believing them, they walked over to the stadium just as the American team was arriving. The team suggested Jim and his friends join them, so Jim told his friends to show any I.D. they had as the Russian official couldn't read English anyway. They marched together with the U.S. team into the stadium. Inside, there were plenty of empty seats, so they melted into the grandstand. Jim told me that there is no way to describe how it feels to see the American flag flying in a foreign land as he watched the bearer of our flag marching down the field.

Life was not easy in authoritarian Russia. Jim was not comfortable sleeping on his soft bed, so he put his mattress on the floor. He was told "That is not allowed!" This was 1970, and Russia was having a drought in the part of the country that raised the food so about the only vegetable available was potatoes. One didn't ask to see a menu in a restaurant as hardly anything on it was available anyway except potatoes.

Jim was a conscientious objector to the Vietnam war, so he applied to the Peace Corps. While in Russia, his acceptance into the Peace Corps arrived with his assignment to Korea to teach English. From the land of potatoes, Jim arrived in the land of rice! Rice every day for three years!

One very interesting letter from Jim arrived from Korea on Ground Hog's Day. Significant because his Dad was born on Ground Hog's Day in 1924 and this was Jimmy's 48th birthday.

"The year 1972---is the Year of the Rat in the Chinese (and Korean) calendar, the first of the 12-year cycle.

> The rat was chosen to be first among the animals who represent the 12 years for the following reason: When he was dying, the Great Buddha called all the animals to his bedside. The cow started out first, faithful as always, but the rat, clever animal that he is, jumped on the cow's back and rode all the way. At the last minute, he jumped down and arrived first at the Buddha's bedside, thus becoming the first of all the animals who came.

---is the year in which you (the eldest son, a very important position to occupy in this part of the world) are 4 twelves in age, and I, your eldest son, am exactly half that, being 2 twelves in age. (It is also interesting for Chinese fortune tellers or whoever, that both of our mothers are also older than we by 2 twelves this year.)

---is the year in which I send you birthday wishes after 12 moons in Asia (and that alone is pretty weird!)"

Since my early interest in the Orient, I knew I was also born in the Year of the Rat and consequently, I have a large collection of rat netsukes I started on my first visit to Hawaii. A netsuke is a small, carved toggle Japanese men hung on their belts. Many are the animals of the Chinese calendar. Most are made of ivory or bone and the owners would rub them to sooth themselves while they were meditating. My cousin, Jean, was born in the Year of the Ox. She and I would exchange oxen and rats. Thanks to her, I have a ceramic rat hiding in the corner by my front door.

The next letter from Jim came from Andong, a six-hour train ride south from Seoul, where he spent the next three years.

Dear Family:

A week in Andong and Korea is beginning to come alive for me. Each day filled with some of the strangest sights, sounds, and especially smells—seems like a week by itself. And so already I feel like I have been in Andong more than a week. Among the little things that struck me and have more than once caused me no end of chuckles and try to convince myself I am really doing this.

A tiny woman layered in clothes walking nimbly down the muddy road, supporting a huge porcelain pot, at least half as tall as herself on the head, suddenly spots me approaching. Absolute confusion as she can't decide whether to stop and put down the load so she can stare at me. And the old guy with her in the horsehair hat, gray robe, a long white beard, who does stare. They think I look funny?

Twenty-five straight meals with rice—and no end in sight. And it's not just a bite of rice—a whole bowl. Thank God I like the stuff. In two years, that's 2,190 meals of rice!

Forgetting my toilet paper one day—a real catastrophe as often there is nothing to use—learning Koreans consider it very unsanitary to blow the nose in a handkerchief and then putting it back into your pocket (it probably is) and then witnessing their method: right out the nose into the street. Witnessing the morning ritual of washing hands and face: much like a bird bath, water all over the place, very little accomplished in this boy's opinion. Ordering chicken, rice and tea and getting soup and tea. Finding out my co-teacher, who has been teaching English for ten years speaks no English—accepting invitations to three different homes without ever knowing I had accepted one!

Today I was walking along, and I couldn't figure out why this terrible smell stayed with me as I walked block after block. I finally spotted the two "barrel men' in front of me—they are the ones who empty out the outhouse holes, and their barrels, balanced on their shoulders on a long rod, were full. They use this for fertilizer. (end of letter)

In 1973, I traveled with my mom, her husband, Les, and my sister-in-law Betty's mother, Irene, to Korea to visit Jim. Jim sent me a letter with a short lesson on reading Korean I was supposed to study on the airplane before our arrival. When we landed at Seoul, Jim met us, and he pointed to a sign in Korean on a nearby building. He said, "Mom, what does that sign say. I sounded out "ice cream" and he said: "Right, Mom, that is what it says."

The Korean language looks like geometry to me ... quite different from Japanese and Chinese. It was invented by a man in 1600. Each little line is a sound, so it is just a matter of sounding out the word; whereas, Chinese is a picture language.

Our little entourage, accompanied by Jim, boarded a train for Andong, sharing the ride with goats and chickens and Koreans with laps full of all kinds of things. They were fascinated by our appearance and wanted to talk to us, but they needed to know how old we are. Jim explained that in order to address people, they must know how old they are. They flooded us with questions which he translated. Jim said this could be the highlight of their life as Americans were rarely seen in Korea.

Our stay in Andong with Jim's Ajumoni (his landlady) was a true Korean experience. We slept on the floor and during the day, it was "sit" on the floor on one-inch grass mats. A cupboard which held the bedding during the day and a low table were the only furniture. There was one windowsill deep enough to sit on. We would take turns resting our backs and legs. The "outhouse" was located outside next to the property wall where it is handy for the "barrel men" mentioned above. Not a fun experience in the middle of the night.

The Ajumoni's kitchen consisted of a four-foot square hole with a dirt floor in the middle of the main room. She would stand in this hole cooking and peeling delicious pear apples for us. When we arrived, there were three chickens in the backyard. We enjoyed their eggs until we heard the last squawk coming from the backyard announcing our last chicken dinner was about to be prepared.

Walking to the market, a long row of stalls, we realized we were being followed by several curious people. The first stall was a man frying worms in a big pan with many children watching and waiting, because they love them. Jim said they grow out of this desire as they get older.

In the middle of the main intersection, a uniformed man stood on a pedestal directing traffic which consisted of a man pulling a cow on a rope and a few bicycles. Returning, Jim took a picture of me directing "traffic".

Notice, the traffic is one bicycle. The old man behind me is wearing the traditional robe and horse-hair hat.

Our water for drinking was made by boiling barley because the water took on a certain brown color. This was the guarantee that it was safe to drink. One evening, we had a pleasant time at a tea house, drinking barley water and listening to classical music. One could tell the size of a town by how many tea houses (a one-tabang town or a two-tabang town) were there. I realized, in Southern California, we could tell the size of a town by how many freeway-exits it had.

By the time we visited Jim, he was no longer teaching 600 11-13-year-old students. Instead, he traveled the countryside teaching the English teachers to speak English as most of them could only read it. We took a merry bus ride over a bumpy road to attend one of his group lessons. Jim put all of us up on a stage and then asked the teachers to ask us questions. The first question asked of me was "How old are you?" I answered that in America, no woman will admit her age.

At dinner, we sat on the floor around a long table with all the teachers. Jim had told me that Koreans love to sing, especially after they have had a few drinks. He told me how to say: "Let's sing" in Korean. This really cracked them up and one tiny little teacher (most Koreans didn't come up to Jim's armpits) said: "Let's sing "Old Black Joe!" Then I cracked up! This song was a no no in the United States, since the Civil Rights movement.

What we discovered was the Koreans had learned all these old songs from missionaries. Most of the songs were from my mother's youth, such as "Bicycle Built for Two" and "Home on the Range."

Jim told us that one of his teaching methods was for the teachers to put on plays for the students. The Three Little Pigs was one they acted out and Jim had mischievously picked the tiniest teacher to be the Big Bad Wolf.

Another letter from Jim came years later from Lima, Peru. He was attending the University of California at Berkeley working on his doctorate in Lima.

Lima, 15 December 1986

Dear Friends and Family, especially Grandma Lola and Les:

Christmas-fiesta approaches and with it, the beginning of summer in the South of our world. Much around me in Lima really does make me feel like I'm standing on my head looking at the world from a different angle: a world where the desperately poor are the vast majority and not a too-easy-to-forget fraction; where it never rains but is damp and grey almost all of the time; where cultures and ways of life separated by centuries and continents clash every day in the streets even though everyone is "Peruvian," "Catholic," and a "child of God"; where theology is inevitably politics and politics the incarnation of faith; where everything important happens in Spanish (except my private pleas to God).

Not all is unfamiliar in these surroundings: friendship is born and grows, often unexpectedly, a mystery, but always welcome; reality turns out to be a good deal more complex than a first (or second or third) glance would indicate; and life is time spent loving God—and washing clothes, preparing food, sweeping my room, travelling on buses, attending meetings.

Seven months of the unexpected and the ordinary in Lima. I arrived at the end of May, plans in hand for a year's research and writing on liberation theology in the "movement's" birthplace. Last April a careful reading of the major texts seemed a good preparation. Yet could one ever be "ready" for Lima where the texts' frequent references to "an unjust and oppressive social reality" turn out to be an overwhelming panorama of human misery and death in all its forms? I guess I could not have been "ready" to face the question of who God is in Lima—loving, just, present? A disorienting and dark question—and (at least for me) one not settled simply, once and for all.

But neither could I have anticipated Gustavo Gutierrez's invitation in late July to move to the parish where he lives and works—a move which rescued me from the anonymity of Lima's vastness, put me smack dab in the ambiente of the theological master himself, and offered me instant pastorship (Peruvian style—community leads the way) of the church of Cristo Redentor during Gustavo's lengthy absences. Talk about standing on your head. Nicest of all is the gradual inter-weaving of lives in which one ceases to be a menacing stranger and instead becomes, with all my particularities, just another brother in a family of special people.

It is no news that life is a struggle and frequently painful, even if truth, justice, and love are worth the fight. What I already knew has only been confirmed in Lima. Yes, it is news—good news—every time people find a way to celebrate, to party, to feast along the way, even amid the sorrows. People here, like people at home, have the gift of fiesta. More than an escape from a world where life is threatened on every side, fiesta is the re-creation of life at the heart of this world. FELIZ NAVIDAD—Happy Re-birth. Here's to you across the miles!

Lots of Love,

JBN

Pretty heady stuff to receive at Christmas Time. For several years Jim's schedule was six months in Peru and six months at Berkeley. When in Peru, our only way to converse with Jim was through a lady in Kansas who had a short-wave two-way radio. We would call her, and she would contact Jim in Peru.

After a couple years of this schedule of winter months in Berkeley followed by the winter months in the Southern Hemisphere, Jim sounded so depressed to me. I told him he was a California boy and needed sunshine. When this schedule ended, he did recover. Jim had added Spanish to his knowledge of Russian and French.

Dated 8 Nov. 2010, Jim presented me with Gustavo Gutierrez Essential Writings, James B. Nickoloff, Editor

Jim's knowledge of Spanish aided Gustavo in his writings. I met Gustavo, a very short individual as he had suffered from polio as a child. He is a big man in personality, and I am happy to say he is in his Platinum Years at 92.

I should tell you Jim joined the Catholic Church when he was teaching in Korea. The local Korean Catholic Church planted a magnolia tree in his honor. I wouldn't have been surprised if Jim had come home a Buddhist from Korea, but I was surprised he had become a Catholic.

Jim joined the Jesuits in Boston and was assigned to teach in Jamaica, eventually being ceremoniously ordained a diaconate and then, a month later, ordained a priest at Holy Cross in Worcester, Massachusetts. He taught Catholic systematic theology from 1989 to 2009 at Holy Cross where he also took part in the Latin American Studies, Peace and Conflict Studies and Women's and Gender Studies programs.

No longer a priest, Jim is a retired Associate Professor Emeritus of the Department of Religious Studies at Holy Cross. He has also taught at Boston College, Weston Jesuit School of Theology (Cambridge, MA), Santa Clara University, currently every summer (in Spanish); the Jesuit Theological College (Melbourne, Australia) several months every year, and the Catholic Theological Union (Chicago). He is currently Director of Ministerial Formation in the Department of Theology and Philosophy at Barry University (Miami Shores, FL). When Jim retired from Holy Cross, he and his partner Robert McCleary moved to Miami Beach with the promise that he would never again live where there aren't palm trees. (This, after shoveling snow, all those years in Boston.)

When Jim left the Jesuit order, he remained a professor at Holy Cross, but now he was getting paid a salary. He opened his first bank account. The clerk wanted to know where he had banked before. When he told her, this was his first bank account ever, she couldn't believe him. All those previous years with the Peace Corps and then the Jesuits, he had received just enough money to keep him in a toothbrush and basic necessities.

In 2020, Jim edited a book recently published: In, Out, and About on The Hill, LGBTQIA+Alums Reflect on Life at Holy Cross, 1978-2018.

I am going to take this opportunity to push my own memoir, *Grossly Outnumbered*: Life and Times of a mother of five Baby Boomers, all Boys, I wrote and published in 2009, (my Golden Years!) It is available on Amazon along with four *Granny with the Freckled Knees* books I wrote for children between the ages of six and nine. The Granny books are about Thailand, Egypt and two on Africa published in 2017.

Back to my subject: letters. No.2 Son John (he changed his name legally to Jon) wrote a very long letter from Iquitos, Peru. He was on an expedition by himself to the jungles near the head of the Amazon River to collect fern spores in 1970. His college major was botany and he was a joy to walk with because he could tell you about every tree, leaf and bud.

Sunday, November 26, 1972

Happy Thanksgiving!

I missed it down here. In fact, I didn't even remember it until today. It doesn't seem like anything but tropically lazy days in Iquitos. It is about 1:30 p.m. and there is not a soul on the streets. Every day during the week the stores close from 12 to 4, the hot part of the day. On Sundays all the stores are closed and even the rats go underground.

Iquitos is a muy lindo (very pretty) town especially when you compare it to Pucalpa or Tingo Maria. The streets are paved, and it is about the first time I've been on solid ground since I've been in the jungle! The city has grown largely because it is on the portion of the Amazon River that is navigable by ocean freighters. At Iquitos the river is probably over a hundred feet deep!

I will send you this letter as a diary of my experiences so far going back to:

Monday, November 20, 1972. Tingo Maria.

Today Jose Loyase Torre showed me the University de Agraria de la Selva where he teaches. The University was small, containing only four buildings for instructions, a green house, homes for the professors, a small natural history museum, and a library. The library contained very few books although it did contain a partial collection of the Chicago Natural History Museum works on Peruvian flora. Most books were in English. Jose wanted me to find out if there is any information on the Genus Pteridium in relation to the extraction of silica in the stem. Walter, another professor, was the only one who could speak English and he offered me assistance in any way that I might be able to use the University's resources. Ernesto Nunez de Prado and his wife (IBM technical advisor in Peru) and I spent the remaining day discussing the Peruvian culture.

Tuesday, November 21, 1972

I gave Jose my specimens and spores to be sent back to Los Angeles. I gave some small orchids and a bromeliad and the butterflies to Ernesto for them to take back to Lima. I packed my gear and Ernesto took me to the bus station.

Rain at night from 12 to 8 a.m. Temp. 80 degrees Max. Temp. 68 degrees Min. I boarded a bus for Pucalpa. My trip by bus from Tingo Maria to Pucalpa was probably the most amazing trip I have ever taken in my life. The bus leaves late as they are working on the road all day and the road is only open from 6 p.m. until 6 a.m. What is even more amazing is that they call it a road! Between the two cities it is one of the wettest spots in all of South America.

The bus was packed when we started, but that didn't stop the bus driver from picking up another twenty people along the road. The bus reached the road construction and trucks in front of us were stuck in the mud. I didn't speak much Spanish and nobody on the bus spoke English, so it was hard to figure out what was going on. Through all the commotion, I realized that the bus driver wanted us to evacuate the bus while he tried to negotiate a maneuver around the trucks along the edge of this cliff. An old lady, apparently exhausted from the trip so far, and a couple of adventurous individuals stayed in the bus while the rest of us hopped out. We didn't go far, though, and instead promptly sank into the mud about three feet. Everybody was screaming and yelling, and it was dark and raining. What a mess!

I went over to a lady who had sunk up to her waist in mud. At one time she had very nice stockings and white high heeled shoes. But now, she just looked red mud from shoulder to feet. Eventually, we all realized we couldn't go around the trucks by going up the hill because the soil was entirely too soft, so we sloshed along the road and sank only a foot or two.

We finally made it to the bus which by this time, by some miracle, had made it past the trucks. The few who had stayed on the bus laughed and jeered at us as we slopped around in the mud, but it looked to me like they had a few new grey hairs themselves. Everybody breathed a sigh of relief as they got on the bus and everybody became a little more friendly though a lot dirtier.

We went maybe five or ten more minutes and came to a landslide over the road. Some of the truckers had been clearing it away and, in an hour or so, we were back on the road again. The over-grown, pot-holed muddy road (the only link the interior has with the civilized world) is amazingly narrow for allowing 2-way traffic. Usually, the trucks stop while we carefully maneuver around them or vice versa.

We proceeded most of the trip at about 5 miles an hour, but occasionally, under exceptionally good conditions, we went ten M.P.H. After six hours (50 miles) we stopped to eat at this dive. Unfortunately (or fortunately) the place was out of food, so we got back on the bus and continued creeping for another three hours into the night.

We finally stopped on the top of this mountain in fog and clouds at another place to eat. (I couldn't really call it a restaurant in good conscience). We ate what mountain people eat (boiled bananas (very similar to hard bread) and soup with a little rice on the side. The soup had a big animal foot in it, and I wasn't sure if it was a lizard foot or some kind of bird. It turned out to be a bird foot; I suppose it tasted o.k. if you like feet. However, I started the trip with a pretty bad case of stomach cramps, and by that time nothing looked good including the feet. So, I had tea and we left the fog forest.

We made it into Pucalpa at six in the morning fifteen hours later (150 miles total and on time!) They only run these trips about twice a week and in a couple weeks there won't be any road left due to the mucho lluvia (big rains).

Wednesday, November 22, 1972

After this trip, I was somewhat hot, tired and dazed, a little sick and in desperate need of a place to sleep. I thought I would stay in a hotel for a day then go to Iquitos, but they were both full, so I just sat on the curb half asleep. I spotted Ramon Ferrera (Natural History Museum director in Lima) breathed a sigh of relief and went off with him to have breakfast. He said he was off to Iquitos later that day and since I didn't really like Pucalpa, I thought it might be a pretty good place to go. I went down to the aeropuerto, but the plane was full, so I dejectedly took a taxi back to town. By this time, the hotel had a room (I use the term loosely) so I just closed my eyes and fell asleep until the next day.

Thursday, November 23, 1972

I woke up though I kept my eyes closed until I got outside the hotel and wandered around the town. I went by to see Jose Pickling (Ministerio de Comercio y Industrio). His name I got from a friend.in Lima. We chatted a little while about the future of Pucalpa and I derived from the conversation that there isn't much hope. There are not any paved streets and not much industry, the people don't do much and it doesn't have anything a tourist would want. Pucalpa does have a lot of foul smells, a lot of garbage, quite a few rats and these giant vultures that comb the streets in the early mornings.

I met these pilots that fly cattle in from Brazil that have been waiting for six days for gasoline to come in on the muddy road from Lima and by this time were pretty bored. We decided to go to a village Yarria Colcher where the Institute of Linguistics is located about 7 kilometers outside of Pucalpa. We drove there and took a boat out on this lake to the Institute. There were a lot of Americans there of all ages. The Institute has been there for 25 years trying to translate Indian languages in the jungles.

I went swimming in the lake and had a good time. In the lake are dolphins and piranhas and all kinds of fish. The piranhas don't generally attack a person unless he sits still, so you just have to keep moving. The natives don't like the dolphins because they are supposed to be bad. They (the dolphins) according to Indian legend come into the villages at night and rape the women. During the day, the men swim in the lake, but the women will only go out in a canoe and bathe by splashing water on themselves. The women always face shore so that the dolphins won't cast a spell on them which is the process makes them pregnant. The weather was hot with occasional sprinkles in the afternoon.

Friday, November 24, 1972

I packed up and left for Iquitos via a jet. I was going to take a boat up the river but the only one took fourteen days and probably fourteen hundred stops. At the time I wanted to get as far away from Pucalpa, so I flew. As I said earlier Iquitos is very nice. I met a lot of American, Australian and New Zealand oil riggers. I have been staying with Enrico (don't know his last name) an electrical engineer who works on finding areas suitable for drilling. He is a Texan and has been living in and around Equitos for two or three years. He knew a man that handles expeditions into the jungle, and I met him today. We arranged for a boat and an Indian guide for me for a week. At that time, I would have presumably found a spot that is suitable for my base camp. The man's name is Moises Torres Viena and his official guide number is 91.

Well, it is off to the jungle now. You might be receiving a letter by jungle boat soon.

Signed (Jon, Tarzan)

Jon's preparation for his jungle exploration included his backpack stuffed with notebooks to keep records, camera, and packets for collecting his precious fern spores. In addition, he had secured from our local Dr. Davis, a supply of medicines to cure almost anything. In one jungle village, he had the opportunity to give to a very sick little girl an antibiotic that cured her. Her father was so appreciative he gave Jon practical lessons in jungle survival. He taught him how to cut down a palm tree to retrieve the delicious hearts of palm. Unfortunately, this does kill the palm tree. He also showed him how to carve a canoe out of a log and sharpen a stick to spear fish.

The letter above was the only letter we received for the next three months. My husband was frantic, but I kept telling him no news was good news. I always said, "Pretty soon, it will be next week, and this will all be behind me." Miss Pollyanna was wrong this time as Jon had tried to cross a river with all his stuff in a pack on his back. The river was flowing much faster than he thought, and he realized if he didn't let go of his pack, he wouldn't make it across. All his clothes, shoes, research work, camera, fern specimens, medicines, everything went down the river.

Jon became a nature boy and formed his philosophy that you are never lost if you are happy where you are. He was happy enjoying the pristine nature to its fullest, until he got very sick. A native found him slumped against a tree. Thank God, he had left his passport and return airline ticket to Miami at a village before he lost his backpack. He arrived in Miami, barefooted with only a shirt and pants somebody gave him. The passport people couldn't believe he had nothing with him but his passport.

Some friends of ours had moved to Miami because he was an entomologist and decided that there were more bugs in Florida than California. They met Jon at the airport and were shocked at his condition. The Mom called me and said she didn't want me to see him until they fattened him up. He was a big person, but he had lost 100 pounds.

Jon had so many talents. He played the piano like an angel, just hum something and he would play it, from Rachmaninoff to the Beatles. He was the accompaniment to any program or fashion show being put on at Pasadena High School. One night, he was asked to play at a big reception for Ronald Reagan when he became President of the United States.

When computers came on the scene, he invented a computer chess game. His profession turned out to be in computers as he set up paperless systems in banks and court houses from New York to San Francisco. A brain tumor destroyed his beautiful brain when he was 64 years old.

No.3 son, Tom, delivered prescriptions for our pharmacy neighbor, Wes Anderson, during his high school years, and was a waiter at an Italian restaurant in Pasadena. After graduating from Pasadena High School, he saved his money and flew to Hawaii and got a job working in a hotel near the best surfing in Hawaii. But that wasn't all he did:

Kaleiwa, Hawaii, December 12, 1972

Excerpt:

I am taking glider lessons over here which I would like to continue. Gliding is also called soaring. And what happens is you get towed by a rope from another plane and then when you reach a certain altitude (2500 feet), the tow plane lets go of the rope and you and the glider just float along without an engine until gradually you just come down and land. It's like you're a bird. It's really quiet and beautiful. It's costing me $10 an hour to learn and it should run me about 2-3 hundred dollars altogether; but I think it will be worth it to get my license.

It looks right now like I am going to stay in Hawaii and hopefully go to school next fall. The tuition fee will be real cheap since I'll be a resident of Hawaii by then. It should only cost me about 3 hundred dollars a semester, which is cheap.

Lihue, Hawaii, November 24, 1973

Well, I finally got back to the place I love. And Kauai is everything I thought it would be, maybe more, even, than I expected. The beauty here is frightening sometimes.

We got ourselves a nice house and it is very close to school so I walk to and from with no problem. Speaking of school, this school is very good. It doesn't offer a lot of assorted classes, but it does have the essential courses that it takes for a liberal arts major. I'm going to be taking Oceanography next semester that should be great. I can't think of a better place studying the ocean than here in Hawaii.

All my love, Tom

Eventually, Tom returned to California and attempted to enroll in Pasadena City College. He was not considered a California resident, so the tuition was astronomical. I was furious because we, his parents, had been paying school taxes forever and our son was not a native of California???

Disappointed, Tom and his high school friend Marco deSilva went to Colorado with a bunch of Marco's Mom's Mexican recipes with the idea of opening a restaurant. Steamboat Village was a small ski resort and already had a Mexican restaurant.

Excerpt: Dec. 1975

Steamboat Village, Colorado

Dear Grandma Lola and Les:

I have been working hard every day at this new restaurant (Mexican food). I walked right into the head cook and kitchen manager position. My buddy Marco who is my partner in everything here developed an infection in his hip and I had to take him to Denver for treatment. So, anyway, I am in charge here alone and it feels great to have a name for a change. First time for me to have people working under me and hopefully, the experience will help me from here on out. No complaints along that line.

As far as living here in Steamboat goes, I'm slowly adjusting to the cold. Only skied twice so far as my job takes a lot out of me. And yes, I'll do some ice skating for you, Grandma, although I don't know the first thing about it. You both take care and send my best wishes to everyone for the holidays. Love, Tom

I couldn't pass this without telling about his Grandma (my Mom's) experience. She and Les had bought a house in Apple Valley to be near us. It had a swimming pool in the backyard. We did have freezing weather in the winters. Mom noticed that her pool was frozen over, so, all excited, she finds her ice skates and puts them on thinking she could ice skate on the pool ice. Fortunately, the little boy from next door came over and tried to walk on the ice and it broke. I should add that she was 90 years old at the time.

The rest is history, as Tom went on to open a restaurant in Atlanta, and eventually had nine La Paz Mexican Restaurants in five states.

This La Paz was in Vinings, a suburb of Atlanta. Recently, during one of Tom's Sunday visits, he told me he always tries to be diplomatic. "If you are confrontational, you stir everybody up and it goes on and on. If you are diplomatic, people are satisfied and that is the end of it. You can go on to something else. Example: someone wants a raise: "That seems like a good idea. We'll have to talk about it." I say what people want to hear."

There are no letters in Jac's file—only this postcard he sent from Camp Bluff Lake when he was a little kid. I notice it was designed by Hanna-Berra who were famous for their cartoons. Hanna was in one of my high school classes. These are the kind of things a Mom treasures! I guess Jac was always in the United States so he would call instead of writing.

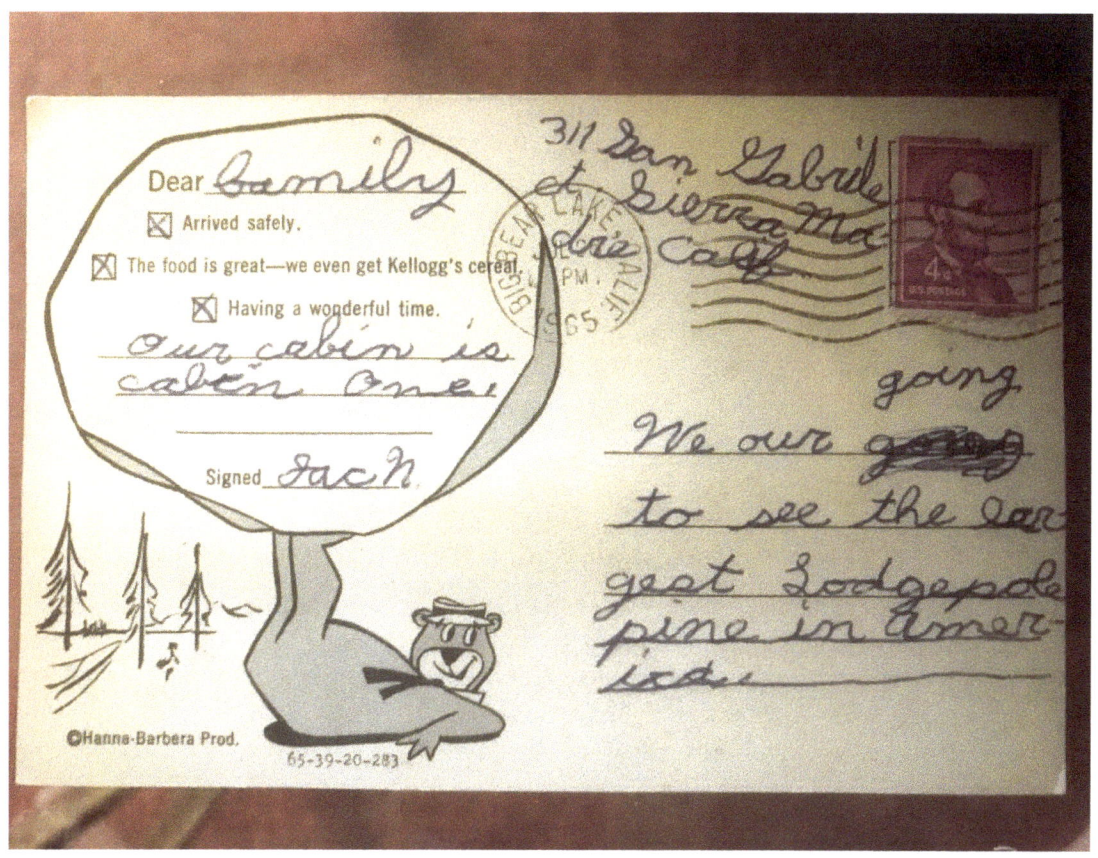

Jac is talking about the old Lodgepole pine that grew near the camp.

Jac has always been a positive thinker. One year in his early teen years, he told me he had a job for the summer teaching swimming at the Jewish Center. When summer came and Jac didn't go anywhere, I said, "I thought you had a job for the summer?" His answer: "I could have had it if I had applied."

I don't know if Jac's stint as camp counselor contributed to his future in science, but I do know he was considering science as early as high school and took Russian, thinking at the time that Russia was advancing in science. He attended University of California at San Diego two years and then graduated from University of California at Santa Barbara. He received his doctorate at University of Colorado at Boulder. His first work on cancer research was done at Harvard, then Albuquerque, New Mexico, and presently at University of Colorado in Fort Collins.

His first published book he presented to his Dad on his birthday, February 2, 1998, signed Jac: DNA Damage and Repair Volume 1: DNA Repair in Prokaryotes and Lower Eukaryotes, Edited by Jac A. Nickoloff and Merl F.

Hoekstra. This volume was followed by DNA Damage and Repair Volume II: DNA in Higher Eukaryotes and in 2001, DNA Damage and Repair Volume III: Advances from Phage to Humans. Chemokines and Cancer, Breast Cancer, Molecular Genetics, Pathogenesis, and Therapeutics, all part of Jac's Contemporary Cancer Research. I did try to read one of these, but it was about "double-strand break and recombinational repair in saccharomyces cerevisiae" and lost me completely.

Jac just received a grant from the Institute of Health in Washington, D.C. to push ahead with his current work looking for new pathways to cure cancer. The two scientists who just received the Nobel Prize were working on the same pathway.

In Tony's file is a Mother's Day card he created when he was in grade school. The 9x12 cover has handmade paper flowers pasted on it. Inside (in long hand): "My Mom She is a good mom, When she is nice, And when I want to play dice, And when she sees some mice, She goes and cries, She is nice, When I want her to make rice. I love Mom Love, Tony Sierra Mesa School Room 8" (Attempt at rhyming?)

I can be rightly accused of being a pack rat as I have many of the Valentines Jimmy gave to me over the years. One of them he handmade himself, a lacy heart, and the date 1986, almost 40 years after we were married. It is so treasured by me that it remains under a glass top on the nightstand.

I wonder if the soldiers in Afghanistan write letters to their families. Probably not, as obviously, now there are other ways to communicate, but they can't be saved and preserved by Moms and wives and friends. Think about it!

I love receiving telephone calls from my sons and friends. Unfortunately, robot calls are driving me and everyone I know, crazy. Surely, something can be done about these robot pests. Invariably, the moment I talk to a real person, he has an East Indian accent. Pushing Block Call hasn't helped as they simply change their caller I.D. They use Tanner Hospital and Southwire and even people's names as the I.D. I have tried telling them I would kill myself if they called again. Not helping. I have tried yelling into the phone as loud as I could. And still, they call two or three times every day—usually when I'm taking my afternoon nap.

As mentioned before, my sons have arranged, among themselves, to call me in rotation every afternoon at five o'clock—my wine time and now dubbed Quarantini Time since the Corona Virus is keeping most of us housebound. The only pre-requisite is to have my glass of wine poured before they call. Son Jim sometimes arranges a zoom call and we have our wine with his friends in Boston or Australia or family in California.

During an interesting Sunday discussion with son Tom, he mentioned he thinks there is a decline in common courtesy. Has the Women's Lib movement killed the courtesies men used to extend to women? Opening the car door or any door for a woman to pass through first was just standard politeness. I could go off on another tangent about women in politics and taking men's jobs and not staying home and raising their kids, but I would be repeating myself.

My husband was taught never to swear in front of a woman and he never did. This could be extended to table manners that were taught in the home. Nowadays, some people sit at the table with a cell phone in their hands, completely ignoring everyone else at the table. I did read about a suggestion for a luncheon gathering: the first one who picks up his cell phone at the table pays the bill. It is almost as though the cell phone is permanently attached to their hand. Remember what I said about becoming a head and one finger in the future. We still have the pen, but for how long?

It used to be the norm to write thank you notes for gifts or sending birthday cards. Even Christmas cards are going by the wayside.

This reminds me of my experience as a senior in high school. I was running for school secretary against two of my best friends. I was flabbergasted when I looked up at the bulletin board and realized I had won the election. At that moment, my bookkeeping-math class teacher, congratulated me and offered me some advice. He said, "Virginia, always remember to write thank you notes. No matter what anyone does for you, always thank them. You will be surprised how many thank yous you receive from your thank yous. "

This little courtesy has paid off so many times in my life and I'm happy to say that my granddaughters take the time to write thank you notes.

Occasionally, my husband and I were moved to write letters of complaint. Here is one my husband wrote to TIME magazine dated: March 21, 1984. I need to preface this with the fact Jimmy smoked until 1974. Lucky me, he never smoked in the house, probably one reason for my longevity. Jimmy was skiing with his friend, Chuck Fuller. He had one cigarette left in his pocket and he said to Chuck, "This is the last cigarette I'm ever going to smoke." And it was!

Mr. John A. Meyers, Publisher
TIME Magazine
Time and Life Building
Rockefeller Center
New York, N. Y. 10020

Dear Mr. Meyers:

TIME has a long history of excellence and I am certain it will continue. However, it is my belief that TIME could take a giant step in continuing and improving that tradition and showing the way to others in the media by engaging in self-denial of certain advertising revenue.

TIME should prohibit tobacco advertising in its magazine!

I understand that the tobacco industry supplies much needed revenue for operating expense and profit to those in your business. However, need alone is not reason enough to accept that money. There should be a consideration of your roll and duty to people.

I would hope and perhaps conjecture, it is possible to replace those tobacco ad-dollars with ad-dollars suggesting to your readers to purchase something of value instead of cigarettes resulting in the inevitable life-debasing effects of smoking.

When I see people smoking; see the advertisements, I hurt, and I have great sorrow for smokers, manufacturers, ad-people or anyone connected with the promotion of the use of tobacco. A religious person might say, "Forgive them for they know not what they do…" Me, I just hurt.

Sincerely,
(signature)
James A. Nickoloff

P.S. If you care to respond in TIME, please do. If you care to publish this, please do. It's free.

The response:

> TIME
> **Time & Life Building**
> THE WEEKLY NEWSMAGAZINE
> Rockefeller Center
> New York 10020

Joan D. Walsh
Editorial Offices
April 24, 1984

Dear Mr. Nickoloff:

Thank you for letting us know how you feel about the inclusion of cigarette advertising in our pages. We respect your point of view, but our decision to accept this advertising is based on the fact that cigarettes are lawful items of commerce. We therefore feel that cigarettes are lawful items of commerce. We therefore feel that the industry should not be denied the privilege – the privilege of all legitimate enterprise – of advertising openly. However, as you may be aware, in our Medicine section we take special care to report fully on the growing statistical and laboratory evidence linking cigarette smoking with cancer and heart and respiratory disease.

> Sincerely,
> (signature)
> Joan D. Walsh

I wrote to TIME magazine August 10, 1998 the following:

Attention: Roger Rosenblatt

Dear Sir:

With reference to your Essay "Talking Race with the President" in the July 20, 1998 issue of TIME, I enjoyed reading your comments about participating in the panel discussion on NewsHour. I watched the original broadcast and several reruns so I wouldn't miss anything.

In your third paragraph you use the word bloviations. Grabbing my handy Merriam-Webster dictionary, I found "blouse" followed by "blow." Not giving up, I took down the first of my two volume Britannic World Language Dictionary. There was "blouse," followed by "blow."

My next resort is always a telephone call to Boston to my Number One Son, who has a PhD from Stanford. He also was unable to find bloviations. Is this a new word or possibly one you have coined?

If it isn't too much trouble, I would appreciate some enlightenment. Words fascinate me and I love meeting new ones.

Forever, a fan of yours, Ginny Nickoloff

I received the following answer dated August 24, 1998:

Dear Ms. Nickoloff:

We can appreciate the fact that the path to the meaning of an unfamiliar word isn't always straight to the handiest dictionary. That was the case for you (and for us, too) with "bloviation (Essay, July 20). But Webster's *Third International* came through; it means windy or excessive oration.

Thank you for sharing your interest in words with us, and best wishes.

    Sincerely,
    (signature)
    Gloria Hammond

Chapter Sixteen
Opera

Dear Reader, I hope you have attended at least one opera in your lifetime. If you attend only one, may it be *Madame Butterfly*. Growing up in Los Angeles, it was shameful the city had no opera house. When building one would come up for a vote, my Dad would vote against it. Operas were forced to be presented at the Shrine Auditorium which also was the venue for the circus when it came to town.

Amazingly, I was on stage in an opera before I ever saw one. While attending U.S.C. with my two girlfriends, Kris and Marilyn, we saw a notice on the bulletin board for girls to take part in two operas coming to the Shrine Auditorium and to be paid $2 for each performance. We signed up!

The first opera was "Aida" with Ezio Pinza. This was a thrill because he was one of the most famous opera singers of the time. Looking him up on Google: Ezio Pinza spent 22 seasons at New York's Metropolitan Opera, appearing in more than 750 performances of 50 operas. Years active: 1914-56. This was 1945. He was a big, handsome 30-year-old Italian. We three and another girl, dressed in diaphanous costumes and Egyptian makeup were to hold a canopy over his head as he marched onto the stage. At the Met, he would ride in on a white horse.

Picture this. Before the curtain is to go up, the orchestra is playing The Star-Spangled Banner and the audience is singing. We are behind the curtain singing with Ezio Pinza! I am still bragging that I sang with Ezio Pinza!

Years later, son Jim took his father and me to the Metropolitan Opera House in New York City for our 25th wedding anniversary. Jim told me to check out the water fountain. It was dedicated to Ezio Pinza. He told us the joke at the Met is to tell someone to meet you at the Ezio Pinza drinking fountain because all of them are dedicated to Senior Pinza.

The second opera of our "debut" was *Boris Godunov*. And we girls were dressed in rags as poor Russians. You may remember Ezio Pinza when he played Emile de Becque in the original Broadway production of "South Pacific. He sang "Some Enchanted Evening" on the original Broadway cast album that made his voice familiar to millions who had never heard or seen him at the Metropolitan Opera House.

I was to find out later my mother-in-law was in the audience at these performances with my girlfriends. She loved opera and had taken my husband to see them when he was young. Jimmy always talked about how much he loved *Rigoletto*.

When Jimmy and I were married, I made him promise if they ever built an opera house in Los Angeles, he would take me to see *Madam Butterfly*. He did take me to the new Music Center in the 1950's and I cried my eyes out watching and listening to this magnificent opera performed by a beautiful soprano. I have since seen it six more times and I cry every time. The last two times, a puppet was used for the little boy and I still cried.

The Metropolitan Opera is now broadcasting live from the Met in theaters all over the world. When the virus broke out, they suspended productions at the Met and did a Zoom with the singers singing from their homes in different countries. It was amazing!

Two of our favorite couples, Barbara and Chuck and Ardie and Dave met us in Santa Fe to attend an outdoor opera. Attending this opera under the sky is a fabulous experience. The opera was *Eugene Onegan*, a Russian opera, with fake snow on the stage and we were sitting high in the stands. The full moon was shining above the stage and, on the stage, two men were pacing off in a duel. I'm wondering if the guns would go off or the moon disappear first. Watching the moon, I jumped straight up in my seat when the guns went off. My girlfriends burst out laughing and I was totally embarrassed as the sad scene played out on the stage.

My next experience at the Santa Fe Opera House was delightful. My cousin, Jean, suggested we spend a week in Santa Fe to celebrate my 80th birthday. I flew to Albuquerque; met Jean and we drove to Santa Fe.

On the plane, I had been reading Opera News magazine. As we were deplaning the girl behind me said she noticed what I was reading. She, Beth Clayton, was returning from singing opera for weeks in the Adirondacks and her friend, Patricia Racette, would be singing in the opera Jean and I were about to see: *La Sonnambula*. At the baggage claim, Beth had about 10 suitcases full of costumes she had worn in her operas. To make a long story short, she invited us to meet backstage after the opera and we had our picture taken with the two opera stars.

If you ever get a chance to see the Santa Fe opera, arrive early and you can take a tour of the eight stories underground that house, the costume making departments, and all the stage sets for the different operas performed.

One of my dreams not realized is to see *Aida* in Egypt with elephants. My mother-in-law saw *Aida* at the outdoor theater at the Metropolis in Athens with elephants!

Are high school students still marching to the Grand March from *Aida* to get their diplomas? Our class had to memorize all verses. The line: "When the tumult and the shouting dies" always occurred to me when I would relax after my sons' birthday parties.

A lovely part of going to the opera is the opera house itself. They are always beautiful with ornate ceilings and spectacular sparkling chandeliers. My husband and I had the good fortune of attending an opera in Vienna when we visited Europe for our 25th anniversary in 1972. I had taken a formal along to dress for this occasion. It was a red gown with a jacket of blue velvet with gold stripes on the sleeves and gold stars scattered over the jacket. I felt like Miss U.S.A. strolling down the red carpeted staircase in this magnificent opera house.

I always dreamed of sitting in a gold box and that dream came true in Budapest in 2002. Bob and I had a gold box looking down just above the stage. Operas nowadays project the translation into English either on the seat in front of you or above the stage. In Budapest, the Italian opera translation was in Hungarian!

Bob and I didn't attend an opera, but we toured the opera houses in Buenos Aires and in Manaus on the Amazon River. In the opera house in Manaus, the audience sat on individual French style chairs upholstered in red velvet. Wood from Brazil had been shipped to France and the chairs were made from this wood.

A highlight of the recent trip to Cuba with my sons was the visit to their opera house. My sons were proud of me climbing the marble staircase to the third level where we could see the statues on the outside of the opera house up close.

Pictured below is the opera house in Budapest where we had a gold box just above the stage. Since this was built in the 1800's, it had an interesting coat check area with rows and rows of big compartments to check the big hats worn in those early days.

Below, the beautiful opera house in Vienna. Ceilings are always beautiful.

The opera house we visited in Cuba was equally magnificent.
See the statues?

Chapter Seventeen
Jokes

Jokes were always a fun part of my life. As a kid, I would read the jokes in *The Readers' Digest* when it arrived in the mail. I would pick one out and tell it to my teacher as we walked out of class for recess. She told me I would be smarter if I spent more time on my studies.

I still think laughter is good for the soul and laughter is good medicine. I hope the jokes I am about to tell will make you smile and maybe even laugh out loud.

Our neighbor would come over with a joke for my Dad. One evening, he told my Dad that a farmer had crossed a pheasant and a duck, but he didn't know what to call it. An innocent five-year-old, I blurted out the answer and my mom banished me to the bedroom and bawled out the neighbor. I knew I had said something bad, but I didn't know the meaning of the word until I was in my twenties. Now, it is almost every other word in the new TV programs. Swear words used to be banned on TV until after 9 p.m. (when children were supposed to be in bed!) Radio is still pretty good about blotting out the swear words and even newspapers are careful but not the movies.

My son, Tony, was a great joke teller and thought about writing a joke book. The best part was most of his jokes were clean enough to tell my fellow bridge players. He loved to ask any old gentleman in line at Walmart, "Did you know that they are now taking three-year-olds into the army?" After his blank look, Tony would say, "But, only in the infantry."

I am going to delight you now with two of his riddles and some of his jokes:

What did the sardine say when he saw a submarine?

    Oh, look, canned people.

What would you get if you crossed an elephant with a rhino?

    Elephino.

Two peanuts were walking down the street and one of them was a salted!

There were two zucchinis crossing the road. One of them got run over. He was rushed to the hospital and the doctor said: "I have some good news and some bad news. He will live, but he will be a vegetable for the rest of his life."

The tomato family were walking down the sidewalk. The little tomato was lagging behind. The Dad shouted "Ketchup!"

Three men were on death row. The first one was taken to the electric chair. The officer said, "What are your last words before we execute you?" The prisoner shouted, "Go Dawgs!' Then the guard pushed the switch, and nothing happened. The guard said: "I guess you are free to go as it is cruel and unusual punishment to do it again." The second prisoner was brought in and asked, by the guard, "What are your last words before we execute you?" The prisoner shouted: "Go Tide!" And, again nothing happened so he was set free. The third prisoner from Georgia Tech came in and said: "If you would connect the white wire with the blue one, this thing will work!" (It helps to live below the Mason-Dixon line to get this one.)

I told this one to a bridge player who happened to be a pastor unbeknownst to me:

Did you know that baseball is mentioned in the Bible?" The answer: In the big inning.

He did laugh.

The next one is classified as a dirty joke, but I finally got up nerve to tell it to three girls at the bridge table and they did have a good laugh.

This cowboy was riding down the road when a big rattlesnake lay across the road. He pulled out his revolver preparing to shoot. At that moment the rattlesnake shouted: "Stop! Don't shoot! I am a magic snake. I can give you three wishes if you don't shoot me." The cowboy said: "Okay. My first wish is to look like Clark Gable." The snake said: "Done!" The cowboy said: "My second wish is to be as strong as Arnold Schwarzenegger." "Done!" The cowboy said: "My third wish is to be hung like my horse." "Done!"

So, the cowboy rode back to his barn and looked into a mirror. Amazingly, he did look like Clark Gable. He rolled up his sleeve and he had huge muscles. And then he said, "Oh, God, no! I was riding the mare.

The third joke is one I've told so many times, my kid's call it: mom's big-mouth frog joke. The story goes: Early one morning, the big mouth frog is hopping around by the pond when he sees a swan swimming around. (spoken with mouth very big):

GOOD MORNING, SWAN. HOW ARE YOU TODAY?
   "I'm fine."

WHAT ARE YOU DOING?
"I'm looking for my breakfast."
WHAT DO YOU EAT FOR BREAKFAST?
"Big-Mouth frogs."
And, with lips tight, the frog says: "No shit!"

On cruises, guests usually sit around tables of six and often jokes would be told. On our cruise on the Danube, Bob and I joined a group of Australians at a table and I was surprised when one of the ladies told the big-mouth frog joke. Had this joke traveled half-way around the world?

Another one in my repertoire is the cat joke. It must be told in person.

A man is driving down the street when he runs over a cat. Feeling very guilty, he thinks the cat probably belongs to someone at that house. So, he gets out of the car and rings the doorbell. When the lady answers he explains that he thinks he ran over her cat. The lady says: "What did the cat look like?"

I would hold up my hands with the palms wide open and my mouth wide open with my tongue hanging out.

One of my all-time favorites is one that was told to me by my stepfather, Les:

These two cannibals were stirring up a big pot of soup. One of them said, "I never did like my mother-in-law." The other one said, "Well, just eat the noodles."

I don't know who sent this next one to me on the internet, but as a bridge player, it tickled my funny bone:

A cleaning lady was applying for a new position. When asked why she left her last employment, she replied, "Yes, sir, they paid good wages, but it was the most ridiculous place I ever worked. They played a game called Bridge, and last night a lot of folks were there. As I was about to bring in the refreshments, I heard a man say, "Lay down and let's see what you've got." Another man said, "I've got strength but no length." Another man says to the lady, "Take your hand off my trick!" I pretty much dropped dead just then, when the lady answered, "You jumped me twice when you didn't have the strength for one raise." Another lady was talking about protecting her honor and two other ladies were talking and one said, "Now it's time for me to play with your husband and you can play with mine." Well, I just got my hat and coat and, as I was leaving, I hope to die if one of them didn't say, "Well, I guess we'll go home now. That was the last rubber."

I saved this funny e-mail sent to me by my hairdresser of 30 years, Morgan Green. She recently retired and moved to Alabama, but she now comes to my house and keeps me looking presentable.

Morgan's Email dated September 08, 2004
Subject: comments made by NBC sports commentators

Here are the top nine comments made by NBC sports commentators so far during the Summer Olympics that they would like to take back:

1. Weightlifting commentator: "This is Gregoriava from Bulgaria. I saw her snatch this morning during her warm-up and it was amazing.

2. Dressage commentator: "This is really a lovely horse and I speak from personal experience since I once mounted her mother."

3. Paul Hamm, Gymnast: "I owe a lot to my parents, especially my mother and father."

4. Boxing Analyst: "Sure there have been injuries, and even some deaths in boxing, but none of them really that serious."

5. Softball announcer: "If history repeats itself, I should think we can expect the same thing again."

6. Basketball analyst: "He dribbles a lot and the opposition doesn't like it. In fact, you can see it all over their faces."

7. At the rowing medal ceremony: "Ah, isn't that nice, the wife of the IOC president is hugging the cox of the British crew."

8. Soccer commentator: "Julian Dicks is everywhere. It's like they've got eleven Dicks on the field."

9. Tennis commentator: "One of the reasons Andy is playing so well is that, before the final round, his wife takes out his balls and kisses them…Oh my God, what have I just said?"

I copied the following from The Atlanta Journal-Constitution dated August 30, 2000 from page 14 of the World Section written by a columnist:

When I heard Ted Turner was going to speak at this gathering with no script (his usual practice), I knew it would be wild.

What does God want? Turner has ideas

Turner made his appeal as he gave the keynote speech to the Millennium World Peace Summit of Spiritual and Religious Leaders, a gathering at United Nations headquarters in New York of more than 1,000 leaders of different religions. Turner, who once called Christianity "a religion for losers," but later apologized, played an important role in convening and financing the summit.

Addressing people clad in ethnic and religious garb from around the globe, Turner talked of his own struggle with faith and issued a plea for harmony and understanding among people of different races and religions.

The speech was vintage Turner—an ad-libbed, vigorous, impassioned performance, delivered loudly and with many gestures....

Excerpts:

On religion:

When I was a little boy, I was very religious...but the thing that disturbed me is that my religious Christian sect was very intolerant—not intolerant of religious freedom for other people, but they thought that we were the only ones going to heaven.

You know everybody—the Catholics weren't going to heaven, the other Protestants weren't going to heaven, the Jews weren't going to heaven, the Muslims weren't going to heaven, would be wild Hindus weren't, the Shintoists, I mean nobody was going to heaven but just **us....** it just confused the devil out of me because I said, "Heaven's going to be a mighty empty place with nobody else there'.

On tolerance:

Basically, we're all the same. We love our children, we love our wives, we love our husbands, we love our religions, we love birds and butterflies and we love flowers and we like to go on vacations, you know. When it's cold we want to put on a warm coat and when it's not we want to take our shirts off. You know, everybody likes to go swimming, just about—you know, most of us.

Anyway, so I thought, well, you know, maybe there is, instead of all these different Gods, maybe there's one God who manifests himself and reveals himself in different ways to different people. You know—what about that, huh?

On race:

First, of all, in World War II, people still thought, some people thought, there were more than one race of man. You know, there was the black race and the yellow race and the red men…but the scientists and the archaeologists have demonstrated that we're just one human race. We're one human race! I mean, it's us!

And we all came from Africa originally and spread out all over the world and then we just— Africa! Africa! Africa! Yeah, man! All right. That's where we all come from.

And we got different colors, you know, because the white people lived in the north and the dark people lived in the south. I mean, that's the way bears are. The bears in the north are white and the bears in the south are black …they're still bears, for Christ's sake!

On nuclear dangers:

You know, we have, I don't know, tens of thousands of nuclear weapons are still pointed at each other in the world today. And they say they're safe! But they can't get the Concorde to take off out of Paris without burning up…All of us together can't get a Russian submarine that's sunk in only 300 feet of water, can't get the people to the surface, and yet they say all these nuclear missiles are safe. Don't believe it. I mean, they're not safe at all.

The only safe thing to do is get rid of 'em! Get rid of them now! Right on!

(End of Ted's quote)

Ted was certainly a one of a kind and I can't thank him enough for creating Turner Classic Movies.

A good friend of mine from California, Joy Lisker, e-mailed me these words of advice:

> We are born naked, wet, and hungry. Then things get worse.
> Always remember you're unique, just like everyone else.
> Never test the depth of the water with both feet.
> If you tell the truth, you don't have to remember anything.
> It is far more impressive when others discover your good qualities without your help.
> If you think nobody cares if you're alive, try missing a couple car payments.
> It may be that your sole purpose in life is simply to serve as a warning to others.
> No one is listening unless you make a mistake.

If you lent someone $20 and never see that person again, it was probably worth it.

Never mess up an apology with an excuse.

Some days you are the bug; some days you are the windshield

If at first you don't succeed, skydiving is not for you.

Don't squat with your spurs on.

Timing has an awful lot to do with the outcome of a Raindance.

A closed mouth gathers no foot.

Eagles may soar, but weasels don't get sucked into jet engines.

There are two theories to arguing with women. Neither one works.

Never miss a good chance to shut up. (I think this is aimed at me.)

Generally, you aren't learning much when your mouth is moving.

Experience is something you don't get until just after you need it.

Don't be irreplaceable. If you can't be replaced, you can't be promoted.

Before you criticize someone, you should walk a mile in their shoes. That way, when you criticize them, you're a mile away and you have their shoes.

The next story I'm going to relate is not a joke, but everyone in my family thinks it is. I have not been able to convince anyone I saw a flying saucer. In this morning's local paper on page 2 is the daily column titled Today in History (July 8, 2020) the following:

ON THIS DATE In 1947, a New Mexico newspaper, the Roswell Daily Record, quoted officials at Roswell Army Air Field as saying they had recovered a "flying saucer" that crashed onto a ranch; officials then said it was actually a weather balloon. (To this day there are those who believe what fell to Earth was an alien spaceship carrying extra-terrestrial beings.)

Remember, I was married in February 1947. At that time, rental housing was almost impossible to get so Jimmy and I put a deposit down on an apartment still in construction. For the six months we waited to move in, we lived at my in-law's house, located a half block off Wilshire Boulevard in Los Angeles.

One day, my mother-in-law Mimi and I were in her back yard when we saw a flying saucer traveling slowly just above the telephone poles. We looked at each other and said, "What was that?" Expecting to hear about it on the news, we heard nothing. We were living with my in-laws from February until August. That coincides with the date the saucer crashed in July, when my mother-in-law and I saw it.

This is my story and I stick by it!

Playing games on the kitchen table is part of Americana. We always played Monopoly on the big oval oak table at our cabin. Sometimes, these games would go on for days.

Jessie introduced me to Mah Jong, and she is always ready to play during our lunch time. We play three games to find the champion of the day. Tony was usually our scrabble winner, but Jessie is amazing at adding on to existing words: men, amen, amendment. She and Tony would come up with new rules to extend the game.

I learned bridge from my folks before contract bridge became the rage. Jon was an expert and had National Bridge Points while playing during his college years. I don't profess to be a good player, but I love the game and I'm suffering withdrawals during the pandemic. I hope I don't forget how to play! I'm also missing the comradery with the bridge players.

Chapter Eighteen
Lists

A list maker all my life encompassed making a grocery list, things to do, and more recently making a list of my favorite movies. I must preface this by saying I seldom watch a movie made after the year 2000 as the language is usually filthy. Son Tony taught me how to record movies weeks ahead on the Turner Classic Movie channel. If I'm not watching the news, or a football, baseball or basketball game, I watch TCM. One rule I have is the TV doesn't get turned on until the six o'clock news unless it is a sporting event.

This list of my favorite movies started out to be 10, but it grew to 21. If you aren't in your Platinum Years, you probably won't recognize many of these:

1. Wuthering Heights
2. Pride and Prejudice
3. Gone with the Wind
4. Moonstruck
5. Some Like it Hot
6. My Cousin Vinnie
7. Random Harvest
8. African Queen
9. My Fair Lady
10. Rear Window
11. Zorba the Greek
12. Elephant Walk
13. Fried Green Tomatoes
14. The Rains Came
15. The Razor's Edge
16. The Russians are Coming
17. It's a Mad, Mad, Mad, Mad World
18. The Great Race (the pie scene)
19. Somewhere in Time
20. Around the World in 80 Days
21. Lost Horizon

I can't believe I didn't put "The Happy Time" as Number One. Proof positive is I have it recorded and will play it for anyone who will watch which means I have seen it at least seven or eight times. Charles Boyer and Louis Jourdan are in this movie about a young boy reaching puberty in Ottawa, Canada, in the 1920's. It is not silent and is very funny. Come on over, and I'll show it to you!

If you haven't seen any of these movies, think about it! Also, think about watching a silent movie. Since I was born in 1924 and movies didn't have sound until 1929, I can remember going to the movie theater before there was sound. The theater in Santa Ana had love seats in the balcony that I used for a bed.

TCM has quite a repertoire of old silent movies. Some of them are real epics of two or more hours. I find myself weeping when the story is touching. Three of Charlie Chaplin's short silent movies have been restored and all are well worth watching for their pathos. Another movie I recently saw on TCM, made in 1928, before sound, is "The Crowd." It is two and a half hours long and the camera work is amazing for that time. Recently on TCM's Silent on Sunday nights, I saw Joan Crawford and Lionel Barrymore in "Sadie Thompson". In 1928, it had problems getting past its suggestive actions and printed dialogue. Sadie gets pinched a couple times in the butt.

That reminds me of a happening in of all places, St. Peter's Basilica in the Vatican. On my first trip to Europe in 1968 with my son Jim, he took me to see the Vatican. When we walked into St. Peter's Basilica, he said he had never been in the church when it was so brightly lit. As we walked toward the back of this immense cathedral, there were bleachers set up and crowds of people gathered as this was a celebration of St. John's Day. The cardinals were walking in single file followed by the Pope. Suddenly, I felt someone pinch my butt. I whispered to my son to trade places with me. I had heard about Italian men, but I certainly didn't expect to be pinched in St. Peter's!

I subscribe to Netflix and have a "queue" of movies I order on e-mail that come on disks. My queue is about 25 movies long and each time I return one by mail, the next one on the list is delivered by mail. You can search for movies by name or by actors' names. This is my list.

Favorite Actresses and Actors

Actresses	Actors
1. Audrey Hepburn	1. Tyrone Power (first love)
2. Kathryn Hepburn	2. Burt Lancaster
3. Claudette Colbert	3. Ronald Coleman
4. Mae West	4. Laurence Olivier
5. Merle Oberon	5. Anthony Quinn
6. Greer Garson	6. William Holden
7. Grace Kelly	7. Jack Lemmon

8. Elizabeth Taylor	8. Jimmy Stewart
9. Jennifer Jones	9. Humphrey Bogart
10. Greta Garbo	10. Clark Gable
11. Ginger Rogers	11. Paul Newman

As noted above, my first love was Tyrone Power. I was furious when he married and didn't wait to meet me first. I used to write to the movie stars requesting a photograph. I had quite a collection including Mae West, Jean Harlow and Tyrone Power, some of them 8X10. By the time I was 14, I decided I was too old for this kid stuff, so I gave my collection away to a youngster.

Living adjacent to Hollywood, one brushes against movie stars occasionally. When I was seventeen, I worked at my first job in the ALCOA (Aluminum Company of America) offices in downtown Los Angeles writing orders for C47 airplanes during World War II. Bette Davis set up the Hollywood Canteen in a building she owned on Cahuenga Boulevard in Hollywood. This was to give enlisted men a free place to go to get something to eat and dance and have fun before shipping out overseas. She asked our office if some of our 120 young girls (all between the ages of 17 and 22) would come dance with the service men. Eight of us went every Wednesday night and went home with black and blue legs. Some of the boys weren't very good dancers!

Bette Davis efforts in working for the Hollywood Canteen. At John Garfield's suggestion of opening a servicemen's club in Hollywood, Davis with the aid of Warner, Cary Grant and Jule Styne transformed an old nightclub into the Hollywood Canteen, which opened on October 3, 1942. Hollywood's most important stars volunteered to entertain servicemen. Davis ensured that every night there would be a few legendary stars visiting soldiers to meet and entertain!

Lena Horn's husband was the band leader. Hedy Lamarr served sandwiches behind the bar. (I think she was the most beautiful woman in the world.) Shirley Temple danced with the service men and, one night, Roy Rogers rode into the canteen on his horse!

My friend Marilyn and I were asked to pose for a publicity picture with a "new upcoming starlet". It turned out to be Ava Gardner. A few years later, Jimmy and I were at the Coconut Grove when down the stairway came Ava on Mickey Rooney's arm. She was on her way to stardom!

I still have a framed certificate, signed by Bette Davis, thanking me for serving at the Hollywood Canteen. By the way, Marilyn is 95 and still living in California. I guess dancing was good for our longevity.

On a date one night, I bumped into Humphrey Bogart and his wife coming out of a night club. She was his first wife, not Lauren Bacall.

When I was sixteen, I won a contest that enabled me to visit Warner Brothers Studio. At that time, the public wasn't allowed on studio property as the movie moguls didn't want the public to know all their little tricks such as when people were riding in convertibles, they weren't moving. The scenery behind them was moving. Cowboys were riding horses in front of painted scenes. Streets were just wooden fronts and, if you watch enough movies, you see the same staircase or saloon over and over again.

On that visit to the studio, I was thrilled to eat lunch at the commissary and Victor Jory and four other cowboys were eating at the table next to us. I also visited the set where Errol Flynn was playing a Navy doctor operating on a sailor. The most exciting part was visiting the "largest sound stage in the world" which had a thunder and lightning storm going on inside with telephone poles strung out over these fake mountains. It was starring George Raft, and only recently did I finally see that movie on TCM and appreciate the lightning storm knowing it was all done indoors.

One night, Jimmy took me on a date to the Hollywood Palladium. We were dancing and suddenly, we noticed people had stopped dancing and were gathered around the stage. Frank Sinatra was singing with his microphone cupped against his ear. That was the beginning of Jimmy's love affair with Frankie. Over time, Jimmy collected every one of Frank's records. My kids hated Frank Sinatra because every Saturday, when Jimmy had them washing cars or giving them a haircut in the garage, he was playing Frank singing "I'll Do It My Way". "Yes,

Dad, we'll do it your way!" Jimmy's secretary gave us tickets for Frank's last performance.

Jimmy opened a restaurant in 1958 in Hollywood on Cahuenga Blvd, next door to the Capitol Records Building. Alfred Newman, the great musician who wrote accompaniments to most of the movies, was one of his customers. He often brought Jimmy his latest recordings and, also any new record of Frank Sinatra's. I still have his big collection of these records, but the restaurant didn't make it.

Just when we had our opening, they dug up the sidewalk to put down the stars imbedded in the sidewalk. In so doing, there was a huge dirt pile right in front of our door! Want-to-be actors in the neighborhood would eat and drink, and then say they had left their wallet in the car, never to be seen again. Unfortunately, there were too many of these "wanabes," so Jimmy went back to his law practice.

The Big Band Era was one of the best things about growing up in the 40's. Dates took me to dance to Tommy Dorsey, Bob Crosby, Benny Goodman, Horace Height, Duke Ellington, and Glen Miller. I got to watch Gene Krupa beat the drums. Recently, I asked Jessie to find Glen Miller's "In the Mood" on her cell phone and I held onto a doorknob and tried to jitterbug. That music still turns me on! When Glen Miller played it, he would stop near the end. We would go on dancing, and then he would start it up again, never missing a beat!

One time at the Hollywood Canteen, a New Yorker asked me to dance and he turned out to be the best jitter bugger with whom I ever danced! The band was playing the "Hawaiian War Chant" and they played faster and faster until he and I were the only ones still on the dance floor. He was throwing me over his shoulders and between his legs. Boys from New York were always the best dancers.

Dancing reminds me of another story. In case you don't know, snoods are a net-thing we girls wore over our "page boy" hairdo's. I was dancing one night with a tall handsome Marine. His watch band got tangled in the back of my snood. What a joke we were, trying to get untangled on the dance floor!

Another even crazier story was when eight of us ALCOA girls were taking our vacation together. We dressed up in almost identical cardigan suits with lace jabots, hats and gloves and high heel shoes. We boarded the Union Pacific Daylight train for San Francisco. We were thrilled to be going to "The City" as San Francisco identified itself in order to lord it over L. A.

The first thing that happened was my friend Kris stumbled getting off the train, falling into the porter's arms and breaking the heel off her shoe. Poor thing, there she was hobbling around on one high heel. But the funniest thing that happened was when we were hanging on the side of the cable car. Oh, I forgot to tell you that we wore "rats" under our bangs and under our page boys. Rats were fake hair to give our own hair more fullness. So, here is Kris hanging on the side of the cable car with her hair blowing in the wind, and the rat flew out of her hair! We laughed ourselves sick as we often did in those days. The weekend in 'Frisco' (they hated that nickname!) was followed by the rest of our vacation in Yosemite. This was the beginning of our great love affair with Yosemite Valley where we eventually got summer jobs.

We did have some crazy songs such as "Three itty fitties in a itty bitty pool. Boop boop, diddum, diddum, wadom chu" or whatever! In high school, the school band would play at the Wednesday afternoon "hops" in the girls' gymnasium, so everybody learned to dance when we were young.

One night, Jimmy and I were dancing at a Hollywood nightclub celebrating one of our wedding anniversaries. Zsa Zsa Gabor and her husband (the owner of a chain of Baker's shoe stores) were also celebrating their wedding anniversary. They had been given a big balloon. Dancing next to them, Jimmy told them we were also celebrating our anniversary, so she gave us the balloon which we took home. It floated against our bedroom ceiling until the helium leaked out!

Another list I compiled:

Most beautiful places in the world:
1. Yosemite National Park
2. Plitvice Lakes, Croatia
3. Lake Tara, Georgia (my lake)
4. Hawaii (Kauai, Maui, Na Pali, Diamond Head)
5. Taj Mahal
6. Kyoto, Japan
7. Okitsu, Japan
8. Lake Bled, Slovenia
9. Taroko Gorge, Taiwan
10. Santorini Island, Greece
11. Pacific Coast Highway
12. Sydney Harbor, Australia
13. Callaway Gardens, Georgia
14. Fairchild Gardens, Florida

My son Jon took this picture of me in my early Golden Years at Callaway Gardens when a butterfly landed on my hat.

Most beautiful cities in the world:

1. San Francisco—from the Top of the Mark at sunset when the lights come on the bridges
2. Rio de Janeiro—from the bay
3. Paris—from the Eiffel Tower
4. Acapulco—from the Las Brisas Hotel at night
5. Miami—from a cruise ship at sunset
6. Hong Kong—from the ferry boat
7. Guilin, China
8. Cape Town—from Cable Mountain
9. Venice—from anywhere
10. Dubrovnik, Macedonia
11. Sydney harbor, Australia
12. Florence, Italy

To help remember things, I use a system my Dad taught me. He was giving a lecture on memory association techniques and he used me to demonstrate. I was about nine years old. First, he had the audience name ten animals which he listed on a black board for me to memorize. Then, without my being able to see the blackboard, he would call out a number and I would name the animal. In my mind, I had associated the number one with "run", two with "zoo", three with "tree", four with "door", five with "beehive", six with "sick, seven with "heaven", eight with "gate", nine with "wine", ten with "den". Even remembering that after all these years shows how well association works.

I had visualized the animal with its associated number, for instance: 1. horse, I visualized a horse running; 2. cow, I visualized a cow in a zoo, 9. monkey, I visualized a monkey drunk on wine. The more ridiculous the visual, the easier to remember because the number recalled a rhyming word associated with the animal. To take this a step further, I used this idea of association when I was studying bacteriology at U.S.C. and, 75 years later, I still remember a Frenchman named, Ambroise Pare discovered the circulatory blood system in 1510, because I visualized a pear with blood vessels running all over it.

A grocery list technique is to spell a word with the first letters of each item on the list. This is handy if you forget to bring your list to the store. "Short" could mean soap, hamburger, olive oil, radishes and tomatoes.

Fooling around one day, I started thinking about:

All the things that have come into being in my lifetime: 1924-the present.

Kleenex	Frozen Food	Alexa
Color photography	Refrigerators	Home printer
TV	Ice cubes	Recorders
Radio	Record players	Amazon
Jet planes	Calculators	Home delivery pizza
YouTube	Velcro	Computers
Spaceships	No-iron fabric	Cell phones
Dial phones	Missiles	Golf carts
Electric cars	Throwaway diapers	Electric scooter
Automatic washers	Seat belts	Blenders
Automatic dryers	Infant seats	Google
Vacuum cleaners	Atomic bomb	Space shuttle
Microwave oven	Microchips	Automatic vacuums
Wall to wall carpet	Backyard swimming pools	Recliners
Weed eaters	Electric guitars	Gas lawn mowers
Electric lawn mowers	Electronic speakers	Electric fans
Dishwashers	GPS	Electric stoves
Electric coffee makers	Drones	Pressure cookers
Air conditioning	DVDs	Remote controls
Bikinis	Jeans (Levi's)	iPad
Email	Foam cushions	Car radios
Car heaters	150mph trains	Talkies
Chunnel (186 mph)	McDonald's	Online banking
ATMs	Walmart	Voice-over

Jet skis	Synthesizers	Tape recorders
8-track recorders	Skateboard	Ski boards
Motorcycles	Hedge shears	Garbage disposal
Cable TV	Walkman headphones	Transistor radios
Credit cards	Women's two-piece bathing suits (1945)	

Maybe you can think of some more.

And, according to Jac, his cell phone is also a camera, an alarm clock, a calendar, a flashlight, a watch, world news, dictionary, a ruler, streams music, books, local news, weather, and soon he says it will start his car and there will be no "touch" technology … just voice command. That is his daughter Brielle's job.

Jimmy's cousin, Stephitza, was visiting us from Slovenia when we got our first microwave oven. She laughed and said we were cooking with our fingers. How many of the above do we operate with our fingers. Remember what I said about a finger attached to a head in the future. With the new voice technology, we won't even need our fingers! How about a head with only a big mouth?

If these many things have come into being in my lifetime, what in the world is ahead in the future?

Things that have disappeared in my lifetime:

Clotheslines	Vaudeville
Streetcars	Big home freezer
Dial phones	Corsets
Party lines	Garter belt
Circuses	Good Humor ice cream truck
Ice boxes	Movie Tone News
Black and white movies	Helms' bread delivery trucks
Black and white graduation pictures	Ice man
Drive-ins with carhops	Milkman
Silk stockings	Shorthand
Women's hats and gloves	Maternity stores
Hats and shoe stores for women and men	Girdles

Silver tea sets	Popeye and other cartoon shorts at the movies
Overalls	Running boards on cars
TV ending at midnight	Soda fountains in drugstores
Mimeographs	Fountain cokes (not bottled)
TV antennas on the rooftops	Dime stores (replaced by Dollar Stores)
Window air conditioners	Gas stations with windshield cleaning and checking the oil for free
Ladies' handkerchief parties	Big bands and ball rooms
Customer dialed long distance (1951)	Letters and thank you notes
Before that, you first talked to an operator.	*(I hope not!)*
Telegraph	

Speaking of big home freezers. We had one in our garage especially for bread as our family ate 20 loaves of bread a week and I bought bread at the Day-Old store and kept it in the freezer.

Things I wish had disappeared

High heel shoes
Bras
Viruses
Robot phone calls
Waiters who say "what do you guys want? (I am not a guy)
Tailgaters
Using the F word in movies
Self-service gas stations
Traffic-stalled freeways
Panty hose
The phone ringing all the day

(I wouldn't mind if it rang for me but it rings for me not. It's only a pesky robot)

Here is my original list of:

22 Things to do in this Lifetime and what I've accomplished

1.	Visit the country of your ancestors. (Germany)	Yes
2.	Leave a dollar where a kid will find it.	Yes
3.	Lend money to a friend without expecting it back.	Yes
4.	Get a designer dress	(Mr. Blackwell and Oscar de la Renta)
5.	Ride a gondola down the Grand Canal in Venice.	Yes
6.	Teach a class (docent at the museum)	Yes
7.	See the sun rise over ruins at Machu Picchu.	No
8.	Plant a tree.	Yes
9.	Fly on the Concorde.	No, thank goodness
10.	Stand on the Great Wall in China.	Yes
11.	Make your own beer.	Yes
12.	See an opera at La Scala.	No
13.	Learn to speak French.	Some
14.	Take a balloon ride over the Serengeti.	Over the Mara
15.	Kiss someone passionately in public.	Yes
16.	Play the Old Course at St. Andrews.	Played the putting course
17.	See the Taj Mahal.	Twice
18.	Own a Jaguar	No
19.	Visit Tashkent and Kiev	No
20.	Visit Mackinac Island	Yes
21.	See the Duck walk in Peabody Hotel in Memphis.	Yes
22.	Ride a merry-go-round (Provence, France)	Yes

Now, make your own list!

Besides being a list-maker, I'm also a quote collector. One of my favorites:

"All life is a concatenation of ephemeralities."
Alfred Kahn, economist.

I asked Alexa the meaning of concatenation. She didn't know! However, the dictionary said it means a chainlike series and ephemeralities means living one day only.

"I don't mind living in a man's world as long as I can be a woman in it."
Marilyn Monroe

"Blessed are those who can give without remembering and take without forgetting."
Elizabeth Bibesco, British author (1897-1945)

"In the time of your life, live—so that in that wondrous time you shall not add to the misery and sorrow of the world, but shall smile to the infinite variety and mystery of it."
William Saroyan (1908-1981)

"Happiness is not a station you arrive at, but a manner of traveling."
Margaret Lee Runbeck, (1905-1956)

My own wish for my readers is to laugh from your belly, run like a child, dance for no reason, smile a big smile, nap because you can, give yourself a hug, feel peace in your heart, and celebrate the wonder of you.

Chapter Nineteen
Politics

Is it safe to talk politics? You might want to skip this chapter. My Dad was a proud and staunch Republican. Every January, he would make a list of ten things he would like to accomplish each year. He would lay the list on the table by his breakfast plate and read it every morning. One of the things on the list was that he wanted to be respected by his neighbors. I asked him one time if he had accomplished all that was on his list. He cheerfully told me he had, mentioning his new Chevrolet for one. I asked him about the respect of his neighbors. He said he felt he had accomplished that because our neighbors were Democrats and they had asked him who they should vote for governor!

I did learn a lesson a long time ago. It was the first time I was old enough to vote for president. I voted for Dwight D. Eisenhower; however, I also voted for Bernadette Doyle for another office. I am ashamed to admit I voted for her because I thought she had a pretty name. The next morning, I was horrified to read in the paper that everyone was surprised she got as many votes as she did because she was president of the Communist Party!

My Dad and I used to argue politics, much to my mother's chagrin. My social studies teacher believed only Sweden had the right government. Dad was furious because she was teaching us Socialism. He threatened to go to the school and bawl her out. My mother restrained him.

Our class assignment was for each student to write his Peace Plan. This was 1941 and Germany was threatening all of Europe. I worked long and hard on my plan and turned it in. The following day, the teacher announced that none of our plans would work so she had thrown them all away. I was furious she hadn't graded our reports and all my work was lost.

I was even more furious, when the new semester started, and I happened to walk into her room and pinned up on the wall was my peace plan!

According to my son Tom, the school plays CNN in the Social Studies classroom of his daughter, Camila. I guess the schools are still indoctrinating the students with their socialist tendencies. I do sympathize with students today, as there is so much more history of wars to be studied since I was graduated— 80 years ago.

Practicing debates in high school, I knew that in a debate, there are two sides. You may be assigned to argue for a side with which you strenuously disagree. Consequently, for many years I have watched PBS news every evening at 6 o'clock. I sit there and fuss and fume as Judy nightly slants the news in favor of the Democrats. I take my frustration out by writing to the Letters to the Editor of the local paper.

I don't have a date on this letter I wrote to the Times Georgian a long time ago, but it is apropos right now.

"It seems so sad that this country of "free souls" is still bogged down by racial unrest. My deceased husband was a lawyer in California and he always wrote in the space for race: HUMAN. Nowadays, this is what we find: Which of the following best describes your ethnic background?

African American/Black
Asian or Pacific Islander
Caucasian/White
Hispanic
Some other background
Prefer not to say

Please tell me why this is necessary. All it does is separate us from each other. Why can't we be comfortable in our own skin and be a member of the human race. So many "blacks" are voting for? So many Hispanics are voting against? If the statisticians would classify us all as people or humans on this planet, the separations, competitions, jealousies, hatreds, would certainly diminish and hopefully cease to exist in a more perfect world. We can be proud of our ethnic backgrounds, celebrate, enjoy and share our differences with each other, but let us not categorize us like a bunch of diverse animals. Let our well-known Southern hospitality offer a friendly nod and smile to passersby, especially if they look different from us. We are all members of the human race. Let's celebrate it!"

Unfortunately, I do have to answer my own question. When I was a volunteer working at the Orthopaedic Hospital in Los Angeles, my job was working in the emergency room. When patients were brought in, I asked them pertinent questions and filled out the record of the patient's visit. The first question was, What is your race? I hated asking that and asked my superior if I could skip that question. She said, "no" as the doctors need to know because black people could have sickle cell anemia which would affect their treatment.

I am very proud of my daughter-in-law who is Chinese and my granddaughter, Camila, who is half Hispanic. If one of my granddaughters marries a black boy, I will be a proud Grandmother in a family that celebrates our likenesses and differences.

Thinking back on those days I volunteered at Orthopaedic Hospital Emergency Room. When an elderly lady was brought in, I would ask her age (knowing that all women lie about their age!) and then ask what year she was born. You should have seen their minds trying to do the arithmetic to make the year come out right with the invented age they had given to me. I knew I was being mean, but I did it to take their mind off whatever their physical problem was at the time.

October 3, 2016, The Atlanta Journal-Constitution printed a letter I sent in headlined **Women Should Be Main Caretakers**.

The present discussion on the government providing childcare has struck a sore spot in this old lady who has been around a lot longer than most (1924). Childcare is the responsibility of the mother.

When communism took over in Russia, they put all the women to work and the children in childcare. This is happening in our democracy.

Nowadays with the availability of birth control, a woman should not have children if she does not plan on being their caretaker. I have no statistics to back up my opinion, but I think if all mothers stayed home and took care of their children, there would be plenty of jobs for men so they could afford to take care of their families. If a woman wants to have a career and a family, she should put the career on the back burner until her children are old enough to take care of themselves.

I realize circumstances vary, but the fact that many families today have both the husband and the wife working, it is no wonder that the children are given everything they want except for the personal "care" they need. Ginny Nickoloff, Villa Rica

Another one of my political letters to the Editor was published by the Times-Georgian on December 28, 2019 headlined: President Trump, Keep Cleaning the Swamp.

The major problem with our government is our representatives and senators stay in office for years and years because they will never vote for term limits. It is up to us citizens to vote them out of office after eight years.

When President Trump offered to clean out the swamp in Washington, he set about doing that. Do the American people realize that Joe Biden has been milking the government purse for 36 years and now he wants additional benefits from a presidential term? Not only has he benefitted, but so has his son.

They are part of the swamp. The fact that our president has not held office before is a big plus. He needs to bring in new blood by going after these old government employees in the different departments. Everyone knows it is the president's job to select someone to represent us in each country, but I love the way he talks directly to the world's leaders...forget the go-betweens! The President's tweets are his way of reaching the American people directly instead of through the biased news. Keep after that swamp, Mr. President!

(This was written before Biden ran for president.)

Currently, the big debate is about tearing down "objectionable statues." Should we burn down the Nixon Library because he was a bad president? No, because it holds a lot of history. Or Mt. Rushmore in South Dakota, or the sculpture on Stone Mountain. If, for no other reason, these two need to be protected and appreciated for their artistic value and the many years it took their sculptor Gutzom Borglum to carve them.

Save Stone Mountain for its history of the South's defeat of its slavery system. This was a war to preserve America as one country with one belief in freedom for everyone. My Great Grandfather fought for the North with the Wisconsin regiment and was wounded and spent time in the infamous Andersonville Prison in Georgia. Thank goodness Andersonville Prison is still preserved to remind us of the horrors of war.

Thank God, "Right" prevailed! But, unfortunately, it took many more years for the South to give up its white privileges. I'm glad I didn't live here then! I couldn't have abided it! I had black friends in California and my best golfing buddies in Georgia were a beautiful black couple, Millie and Bob Wilson, who passed away recently at the platinum ages 97 and 93. I will always treasure the friendship of their son and daughter-in-law, Jim and Merle Wilson.

There is a statue of a Confederate soldier in front of the Carrollton County Courthouse. It was placed there in 1910. My personal opinion is that it should not be torn down but moved to the cemetery where the confederate soldiers are buried.

What if we had destroyed the magnificent statue of David because people protested nudity, or the Sistine Chapel because it was built by Catholics? Europe is better at preserving things than we are. It seems like here in America, we often tear down a building if it is over 50 years old. History can't be changed. It is the good and the bad and art is in the eye of the beholder.

Another debate is about changing the "insulting" name Braves for the Atlanta baseball team along with the tomahawk chop. I remember when Stanford changed its name from the Stanford Indians to the Stanford somethings, I can't remember. I'm happy to say that U.S.C. is still the Trojans! What is with this changing of history? The Braves were the Indian Chiefs, for the very reason that they were brave. So, what is wrong with that? It sounds complimentary to me, not derogatory! Are we going to change our anthem: "Does the star-spangled banner still wave o'er the land of the free and the home of the brave" to the "home of the blacks, browns and whites?"

I wonder if Democrats know that the Republican Party of the United States was founded by slavery opponents at a schoolhouse in Ripon, Wisconsin.

That does bring me to another bone I want to pick. I think the biggest mistake our government ever made was setting up Indian Reservations instead of letting the Indians become every-day citizens of the United States, free to live anywhere. The government gave them some of the most desolate land in the United States making it extremely difficult for them to survive. I don't know how, but I think it is time the government remedied this mistake. This is important. History is the past, and can't be changed, but we can do something about the future.

On a happier note, I love living in a small town with a small-town newspaper. Listed under Crime in Carrol County was this item:

An argument over some jellybeans led to a call to the sheriff's office Friday night. According to a report filed on the incident, a deputy responded to an argument between a 55-year-old woman and a 65-year-old man in Temple. The report said the man and woman had began (their word) arguing over some jellybeans and the woman threw jellybeans at the man. The man then threw a book at the woman, which left a scratch on her leg. The two agreed to sleep in separate rooms that night, the report said.

Chapter Twenty
Extracurricular

Life gives us all opportunities for fun activities and what better time to participate in these activities than one's Platinum Years. In, school my generation had choices for what were called: Extra Curricular Activities. These were often listed as art subjects, chorale, learning to play an instrument, shop for boys to learn how to use tools and auto shop. In high school, we also had a choice of sport activity, cooking and sewing and a few choices in foreign language (usually French or Spanish). I took cooking and learned how to bake biscuits and make Waldorf salad. What a joke that was. Fortunately, or unfortunately, someone gave me a cookbook entitled "Dinner in 15 Minutes" at my wedding shower. My poor husband had to put up with these choices for the first couple years of marriage.

By the time I went to Los Angeles City College, I had enough of "secretarial subjects" and thought maybe I would branch out and try art. I chose a course in "Art Anatomy". I sat, expectantly, in the front row when in comes our "subject matter": a young man dressed only in a jock strap standing on a platform right above my head! And my embarrassment continued when our next model was a nude, bleached-blond woman with black pubic hair. That was a revelation in itself!

A major homework assignment in the art class was to draw eight views, 4 inches tall, of a nude from lying on the floor to sitting and then standing from side view, front view, back view and looking down and looking up from below. My poor mother was my model. The looking up from below was the most difficult. The poor thing had to lay on the floor on her back and put her feet and arms in the position so that I could stand on the couch and look down on her position and draw it (as though from underneath). This sounds like a gigantic project and it was!

I was used to getting A's in everything and it was a shock for me to get a C, and convinced me that an artist, I wasn't! Because of the war, I was able to get a job at 17. So, I put in the next few years using my secretarial skills working at ALCOA and then as receptionist and operating a switch board in a law office and taking dictation in shorthand.

The years passed by with marriage and family and, one day, I guess the need to get out of the house prompted me to sign up for a night school class in French.

Unfortunately, the teacher was a boor. He threatened us in our inability to speak French correctly (just like they do in France). One night, when he was bawling a poor student out for his mispronunciation, my girlfriend whispered across the aisle: "Or off with your head!" We decided to forego French.

My next language attempt was Japanese. That lasted even less time because I couldn't understand the teacher's English, much less his Japanese.

Next, I dabbled in art. At this point, I wasn't trying to prove I was an artist. I just wanted to do something with the little spare time I could muster. First, I visited the Los Angeles, California Museum of Art, better known as LACMA. They had a section of art that could be rented for three-month periods. At the time, I was decorating the living room of the Sierra Madre tract house in turquoise and black … turquoise shag carpet and a black sectional couch. (Black because little boys are generally not too clean). At the museum, I found this abstract painting echoing my colors and rented it to hang over the couch.

Jim opening his birthday gifts on the black couch with the abstract painting I copied from LACMA overhead. John is holding Jac and Tom is in the sailor suit. Later, Jac spilled a whole bottle of Vel, the new soap concentrate, on that couch and the fabric disintegrated. Our couches usually lasted only a few years.

As the three months rental was coming to an end, I thought to myself, I could copy this painting. After all, I did take a 6-month course in oil painting. I did make a pretty good copy and hung it over the couch. Then I tried a few more paintings, one of a Dodger game that hung in Grandpa Jim's barbecue restaurant and another of a horse in the snow that hung over the fireplace in their Palm Springs house. My idea was when the temperature in Palm Springs passed the 100-degree mark, looking at snow would have a cooling effect.

The problem that arose was my painting set-up with the smell of turpentine in the den was offensive to the family and an even more important reason for abandoning my artistic endeavor, was the arrival of another son and the "den" became a bedroom with bunk beds. (I just counted 48 words in the previous sentence. Is that a record?)

Those problems and a lot of other problems were solved when we moved to a big house just as the boys were getting old enough to leave home! It did give me a lot more free time to do my thing. So, what was my thing going to be?

I read in the paper a Chinese artist was teaching a class in Chinese Brush Painting at the Pacific Asian Museum. His name was Johnson Su Sing Cho. The Johnson was probably a misnomer given him at immigration. He was an expert in ancient Chinese paintings and helped museums identify the original artist of a painting. In China, copying paintings is considered a compliment, not plagiarism.

This played into my hands, as I wasn't creative, but I could copy. Dr. Cho would always paint a picture in class, and we would copy it. I painted one huge scroll painting of an eagle perched on a rock for Jimmy's law office (the legal eagle). It still hangs in our living room.

Dr. Cho moved to Canada and when I looked him up on the internet, he has made a great name for himself and still living. He is my age. I had a wonderful two years painting Chinese landscapes. Those pointy mountains actually exist in a place called Guilin, China, where I visited in the 1970's. Even more amazing, my daughter-in-law's family lived in Guilin. I was there ten years before she was born!

Next are some of my Chinese mountains. I have another one I painted in my kitchen. I kept wondering why it looked so familiar. It was a picture of the Taroko Gorge in Taiwan. On that trip to Korea to see my son, we also went to Hong Kong, Taiwan and Singapore. Having dinner in Hong Kong, we wondered why men were boarding up the windows. A typhoon was expected. When we flew to Taiwan the next day, we were to drive up the Taroko Gorge to have lunch. We got part way up and had to turn back as waterfalls were falling over the road due to the typhoon.

These are the five seasons (one for each son).

My favorite, springtime.

Next to the fireplace is the "Legal Eagle" I painted for Jimmy's office on Wilshire Boulevard in Los Angeles. The folding screen on the balcony my son Jim brought from Korea. Lucky for me, he has never had a place to put it.

Our move to Apple Valley introduced me to another kind of art. I met Cheryl Thomson who taught me the art of china painting. When we remodeled the kitchen, I painted tiles, with her help, of a mother quail with her babies following her and the dad bringing up the rear, just like they would walk past our house all in a row. These tiles surrounded the counter.

With Cheryl's help, I painted a manger scene and flowers on little demi-tasse cups with Chinese sayings on the saucer which you would see when you raised your cup:

> Freedom from desire leads to Inward Peace, Lao-Tse;
> One joy dispels a hundred cares;
> Love every day, Live Longer;
> Life without Obstacles Leads Nowhere;
> Friends ~ One Soul in Two Bodies;
> Continue to take chances and be glad you did;
> and my favorite:
> Way to Man's heart through stomach ~ Way to woman's heart through door of fine restaurant! (Ginny Lee's wisdom).

When I started decorating our houses in Oriental, Jimmy said, "What are we, Japanese, Chinese, Korean?" I said, "All of the above." I've often wondered if in some former life, I was Asian as I love the curved roofs, the miniature gardens, the beautiful way the Japanese shape their trees.

Moving to a new tract house in Sierra Madre with no landscaping, the first Japanese thing I did was hire a Japanese landscape architect who made a mound in the front yard and planted Dichondra instead of grass. Infatuated with Japanese design, I added an "engawa," a porch that runs across the back of the house and took up bonsai when a friend gave me one which was 19 years old.

The pool was added much to the joy of our kids and the neighbors' kids. It did add a few grey hairs when I heard voices on the roof one day. Tony and friends planned on riding a bicycle off the roof into the swimming pool. They got caught, but I never knew if they tried it some day when I wasn't home.

In the back, the landscaper made a tiny little garden with a "stone stream" and a Japanese lantern. Tom enjoyed it! I've taken the Japanese lantern with me each time we moved.

I had also taken a class in Japanese flower arrangement with my cousin, Jean. When we remodeled the Apple Valley house, I took out the entry hall closet and made a tokonoma out of it. I asked my friend Marilyn if I should really do this.

She said, "Ginny, you have always wanted one to display your flower arrangements. Do it!"

That was the last of my art scene. In Georgia, extracurricular activity turned to golf and bridge, writing and reading. Granted, at 96, my hand probably wouldn't be steady enough to paint. Typing I can still do and pretty fast, even if I do say so myself! As long as I can type as fast as I can think, I will turn out a bunch of dribbles on e-mail, trying to remember my son Jim's caution, "E-mail isn't a letter, Mom! Keep it short!"

My wish, for all Platinum Years people, is keep up your desire to learn something new: a new word, a new book, a new language, a new art, a new game, a new song, a new prayer, or meet a new friend, try a new food or drink; or sport (if not for real, watch a new sport on TV). Get excited about something! "Life is the art of drawing without an eraser."—John W. Garner, American government official (1912-2002).

Chapter Twenty-One
Books

I guess I shouldn't write this book without writing about books. My Mom was an avid reader and a regular visitor to our local library two blocks from our house. I was twelve years old when *Gone with the Wind* was published. Mom got her name at the top of the list to get it when the library received its first copy. She brought it home and started reading, not to stop until she finished it late that night. Dad and I had to fix our own supper.

Because it seemed to me my Mom read all the time, I practically refused to read. I would fake book reports for school until one day I did read a history book about President Jackson for a class assignment. I was quite astonished to find it fascinating. Taking breaks on my first job at ALCOA, I started reading novels including *Anthony Adverse* and *King's Row* and discovered I really liked reading long books and hated to have them end.

During the years of raising kids, it would take me years to read a book. I thought I would never finish James Michener's *Hawaii* and *The Source.* Another long one I loved was *Pride and Prejudice.*

As a member of the Carrollton Writers Guild, I enjoy reading books by our members. The monthly meetings (not now with the virus rampant) are fun as the members critique and share their current writings and we have lunch together. Check out our website: Carrolltonwritersguild.org

Recently, I joined a Book Club. Each month a member picks a book for everyone to read and discuss at our monthly luncheons. Coronavirus has put a stop to that. *King's Row* was my selection for the meeting we couldn't have. I had read it originally in the 1950's and reread it for our meeting.

Most of the Book Club members are about 40 to 50 years younger than me, so I figured none of them would have read *King's Row*. An oldie but goody and I was going to surprise them with the fact that our President Ronald Reagan played the part of Drake McHugh who has his leg cut off in the movie (and book). Ronald Reagan also played "the Gipper" in the movie about Knute Rockne, Notre Dame football coach in the 20's and 30's.

May I wander off as a memory pops into my head? I was a senior at Manual Arts High School majoring in Commercial subjects: shorthand, typing, business math, etc. The thirty-five high schools in Los Angeles decided to have a luncheon gathering of all the Commercial Majors (600 students) at the Biltmore Ballroom in downtown Los Angeles. A student from each high school met in advance and a boy and girl were chosen to give speeches at a luncheon on the benefits of taking commercial subjects. I was chosen as the girl and dressed for the occasion in hat and gloves (this is 1941).

The boy chosen and I were seated at a head table on a raised dais and looked out on the 600 students in the audience. Also, at the head table were two actors who had played Knute Rockne and his wife in the movie. Pat O'Brien, who played the part of Knute Rockne in the movie sat next to me and tried to put me at ease. A fly landed in my water glass and Pat took his knife and slapped it against his glass. It made a terrible noise, but a waiter came running to see what was the matter. Pat said to me, "That is how you get a waiter's attention!"

Now that I think about it, how odd that our first course was a half grapefruit with a cherry on top. I found this clipping from the Los Angeles Times in my high school Memory Book that is so old it is crumbling. It was just the first of over 40 albums that I put together over the years. We always carried gloves—seldom wore them!

Pat O'Brien also suggested I pick someone in the front row to address when I give my speech instead of looking at that vast sea of faces making me nervous. Somehow, I got through that ordeal, but I never forgot how he got the attention of the waiter. Years later, I was at a Ladies' Golf Association meeting at our club.

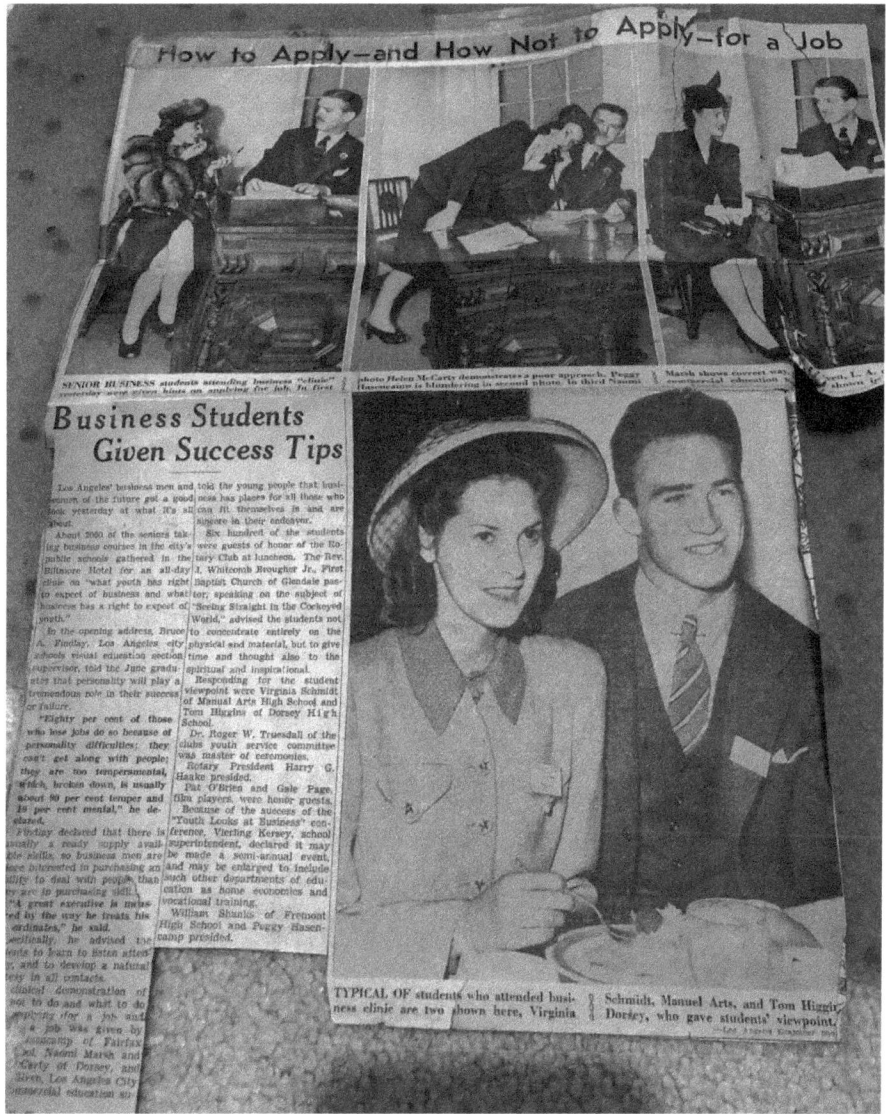

The president was trying to make some announcements, and everyone was talking. I tapped my glass with a knife and complete silence! Try it! It works!

Back to my original subject: books. I have preserved a couple of the books my Dad gave me as a kid. My favorite was *Raggedy Ann and Andy and the Camel with the Wrinkled Knees*. I was so pleased when my Granddaughter Lauren asked for children's books from her guests at her baby shower for Clementine. I immediately got on Amazon and ordered the Raggedy Ann book, and a Raggedy Ann and Andy lamp for the nursery. I was a bad little girl one day and put my *Raggedy Ann* book on edge and sat on it. It broke the cover in half, but I still have both halves.

My other treasure is *Little Black Sambo* given to me for Christmas in 1931 when I was seven. Checking on Amazon for *Little Black Sambo*, I discovered one old copy was for sale at $200. My copy was published in 1908. I saved an article from the Atlanta Journal from 2005:

CONTROVERSIAL BOOK POPULAR IN JAPAN

A reissue of "Little Black Sambo," an illustrated children's book sometimes labeled racist, is back on best-seller lists in Japan. "Sambo,' by British author Helen Bannerman, was first published in 1899. It was a favorite of Japanese families from the time it was introduced in the country in 1953 until it was yanked from bookstores in 1988 during an anti-racism campaign. Zuiunsha, a small Tokyo publisher specializing in reprints, reportedly has sold 95,000 copies in two months since bringing out "Chibikuro Sambo," which is among the top five adult fiction best sellers at major Tokyo book chains.

My brother-in-law, married to Jimmy's sister, started a chain of restaurants serving pancakes in Santa Barbara. My restauranteur father-in-law laughed at Newell's idea saying: "How can he make money out of flour and water?"

The restaurants were called Sambo's, a combination of Newell's partner's first name, Sam and bo from his own last name, Bohnett. He used the Sambo story in his advertising because the last sentence in the book says that "Little Black Sambo ate a Hundred and Sixty-nine pancakes because he was so hungry." Newell portrayed Sambo with a turban explaining he was from India. On page 28, I quote from my Sambo's book:

And the tigers were very, very angry, but still they would not let go of each other's tails. And they were so angry that they ran round the tree, trying to eat each other up, and they ran faster and faster, till they were whirling round so fast that you couldn't see their legs at all.

"And still they ran faster and faster, till they all just melted away, and there was nothing left but a great big pool of clarified butter (or "ghi," or ghee as it is called in India) round the foot of the tree.

Newell was right about Sambo being Indian. Newell eventually had 33 Sambo's Restaurants in California alone and I remember when he opened the 1,000th one in New England. As his company spread to the South, the name Sambo's created many lawsuits as they still thought of "Little Black Sambo" as being racist.

My little book, 5 x 9 inches, has two stories in it. The second one is about slavery, The Story of Topsy from Uncle Tom's cabin. It is truly a sad story about a little black girl who was purchased to be a friend for a little sick white girl who eventually dies. It is indeed very sad, but in my child's mind I always remembered when the old white lady asks Topsy,

"Have you ever heard about God, Topsy?" asked Miss Ophelia, but the child had no answer. She didn't know what the good lady meant. "Do you know who made you?" "Nobody, as I know on," replied the child; "I 'spect I jest growed."

That was the line that stayed with me over the years. This is truly about slavery and not a book I would give my grandchildren. But I still treasure my copy.

A book that had a great effect on my life is *North to the Orient* by Anne Morrow Lindbergh. From the time I read that book, I was possessed with the idea of seeing the Orient. Another of her books, *Gift from the Sea,* is a favorite of mine.

While still living in Sierra Madre California, I invited my high school girl friends to spend a week in Palm Springs at my father-in-law's vacation house. The idea was a complete relaxation … no meals to cook … no washing to do … no kids to take care of …. My friend, Elizabeth Little, needed this vacation as much as I did as she also had five sons. The husbands could not join us until the weekend. After two days, Elizabeth was feeling so guilty that she wanted to go home. I gave her *Gift from the Sea* and told her to read it before leaving. That did it! She stayed the whole week and stopped feeling guilty.

While looking up a list I knew I kept of operas I had seen (75), I found a list of 28 books I wanted to read. This list was dated 1993. I think my Platinum Years are perfect to finish checking off this list. + means I read the book.

The Scarlett Letter		Of Mice and Men	+
Huckleberry Finn	+	The Old Man and the Sea	+
The Great Gatsby	+	Pride and Prejudice	+
Lord of the Flies		The Red Badge of Courage	+
Great Expectations	+	Romeo and Juliet	

Hamlet		Death of a Salesman	+
To Kill a Mockingbird	+	The Poisonwood Bible	+
The Grapes of Wrath	+	And the Ladies of the Club	+
The Iliad and The Odyssey	+	Acts of Faith	+
Wuthering Heights	+	Leopold's Ghost	+
Catcher in the Rye		The English Patient	+
The Crucible		Naked Came I	
Gulliver's Travels		Olivia and Jai	+
Julius Caesar		Something of Value	+

Unfortunately, because my Dad was transferred, I went to school in Long Beach through the 6th grade; 7th and 8th grade in Los Angeles; 9th grade in Long Beach; and High school in Los Angeles. Shakespeare was taught in different grades in the two cities; therefore, I missed Shakespeare altogether.

I did read James Joyce: *Ulysses* while attending U.S.C. Our teacher was madly in love with this book and loved to read passages to us. Unfortunately, he made a funny noise with his throat while reading. Years later, upon meeting a man who also had him as a teacher, we compared notes and sounds and had a good laugh. I remember nothing of *Ulysses*.

Also included in my book of lists was one entitled: Leading Authors:

Mark Twain	William Falkner
Nathaniel Hawthorne	Thomas Hardy
Ernest Hemingway	Henrik Ibsen
Charles Dickens	Herman Melville
William Shakespeare	Emily Bronte
John Steinbeck	Stephen Crane
F. Scott Fitzgerald	Arthur Miller
Jane Austen	J. D. Salinger
Joseph Conrad	Jonathan Swift
George Orwell	Homer

This list makes me feel how inadequate my reading has been. If I live to 103, maybe I can cross off a few more of these authors. It is always nice to have a goal.

I have mentioned my love of elephants but this chapter on books reminds me of the book I recently read by Dame Daphne Sheldrick: *Love, Life and Elephants*. She and her husband established a home for orphan elephants in Nairobi. In her chapter about rhinos becoming extinct in Africa, she was telling about the Pope visiting Nairobi to bring attention to this fact. She tells how they brought a baby rhino from Lewa Downs and dressed its caregiver in white robes so that the baby wouldn't be nervous when the Pope arrived. I put the date and place together and realized that this was the same 30-day old rhino that I fed a bottle of milk when Bob and I were leaving Lewa Downs in Kenya in 2007.

Chapter Twenty-Two
Words

Books are made up of words and, after learning the meaning of bloviate, this windbag is going to put her two cents worth into a discussion of words. I don't think I would be far off if I said most writers love words. One I love is sesquipedalian meaning a long and ponderous word. I haven't used it yet.

One must remember words can hurt, heal, excite, frighten, and enlighten so use them with care.

Every now and then, I come across a word that intrigues me. Years ago, I tried to figure out a way to use the word ubiquitous. I loved the sound of that word, but how to use it? Finally, arriving in Georgia, I could say "the ubiquitous Baptist Church" as they are on almost every corner in Georgia.

Recently, the local paper had the word "biophilic" in a headline. What a great word, but what does it mean? Google tells me it is defined as the inherent human inclination to affiliate with nature. This takes me back to prayer as I look at the clouds in the sky, the trees, the flowers, and the birds could only be here through the hand of God. Is not affiliating with nature affiliating with God? Now, if I could figure out how to use biophilic.

Reading my son's theology dictionary, I came across this fascinating word: phenomenological. Try rolling that off your tongue. I realized it is just phenomenon and logical and quite fun to say.

Here are a few words I have looked up. I'm not saying I remember the meanings!

Cosmogony, convolutions, apotheosis, verisimilitude, peregrinations, internecine, prosaic, truncated, fortuitously, eclectic, corpulent, ethos, esoteric, enigmatic, prodigious, didactic, sacrosanct, perfunctory, philology, renascent, efficacy.

My two favorite sayings that have helped me through a lot of decision making:

Do you have the patience to wait 'til your mud settles, and the water is clear?

Can you remain unmoving 'til the right action arises by itself?

Try these the next time you come to an intersection in your life and you must make a decision.

I read my horoscope every day and saved favorable April 2, 2006:

"You're good at a lot of things, table tennis, map reading, coloring inside the lines, picking up useful phrases in foreign languages, dividing portions equally, predicting the future based on lessons learned in the past. Another thing you are good at, is keeping in touch with people you care about and letting them know in all kinds of creative ways, that you care."

My prowess at ping pong is well known, as well as dividing cake. One son cut the piece of cake and the other one had first choice! N'est-ce pas?

At one time I could count to ten in French, Spanish, Chinese, Swedish, and German. Also, I have a list of telephone numbers of old friends I call periodically. Unfortunately, the list gets shorter as I lose these aging friends. Jimmy's cousin, Carl always called Jimmy on his birthday and vice versa. Since Jimmy's passing, Carl calls me on Jimmy's birthday. Also, he calls occasionally, accidentally, as my number is close to the one he calls often. It is always fun to talk to him as we have great conversations about politics. Great because we agree!

Another friend I call regularly is Marilyn Richter in California whom I have known since we were seventeen and worked together at ALCOA. She is one who went to the Hollywood Canteen and Yosemite with me and then served as my maid of honor at my wedding. It is always fun to talk to her as we have shared memories that go back almost eighty years! Marlyn (without the "I" in the middle) is the girl that married Jimmy's cousin Art and introduced me to Jimmy. She just passed away the day before her 96th birthday. Kris died very young. I also call Evy who lives in Oregon. I've lost track of Betty. Below, we six girls from ALCOA on the beach at Long Beach having fun on a Fourth of July holiday weekend (1943).

Kris   Marilyn   Marlyn   Betty   Ginny   Evy

Chapter Twenty-Three
Genealogy

Interest in genealogy has now reached an all-time high. My mom got into it fifty years ago. It was accidental when she was visiting a relative in Kansas City. This family had just found a family tree in their attic and amazingly, it had Mom's relatives on the tree.

The Thomson Family tree covering six generations 1730-1890.

I have this tree hanging in my hallway and, also, the Seeley Lowry family tree which covers eleven generations 1653-1975 researched and compiled by Lola

Virginia Schmidt Cross (my mom). Designed and hand-printed by Leslie Cross (my Mom's second husband.)

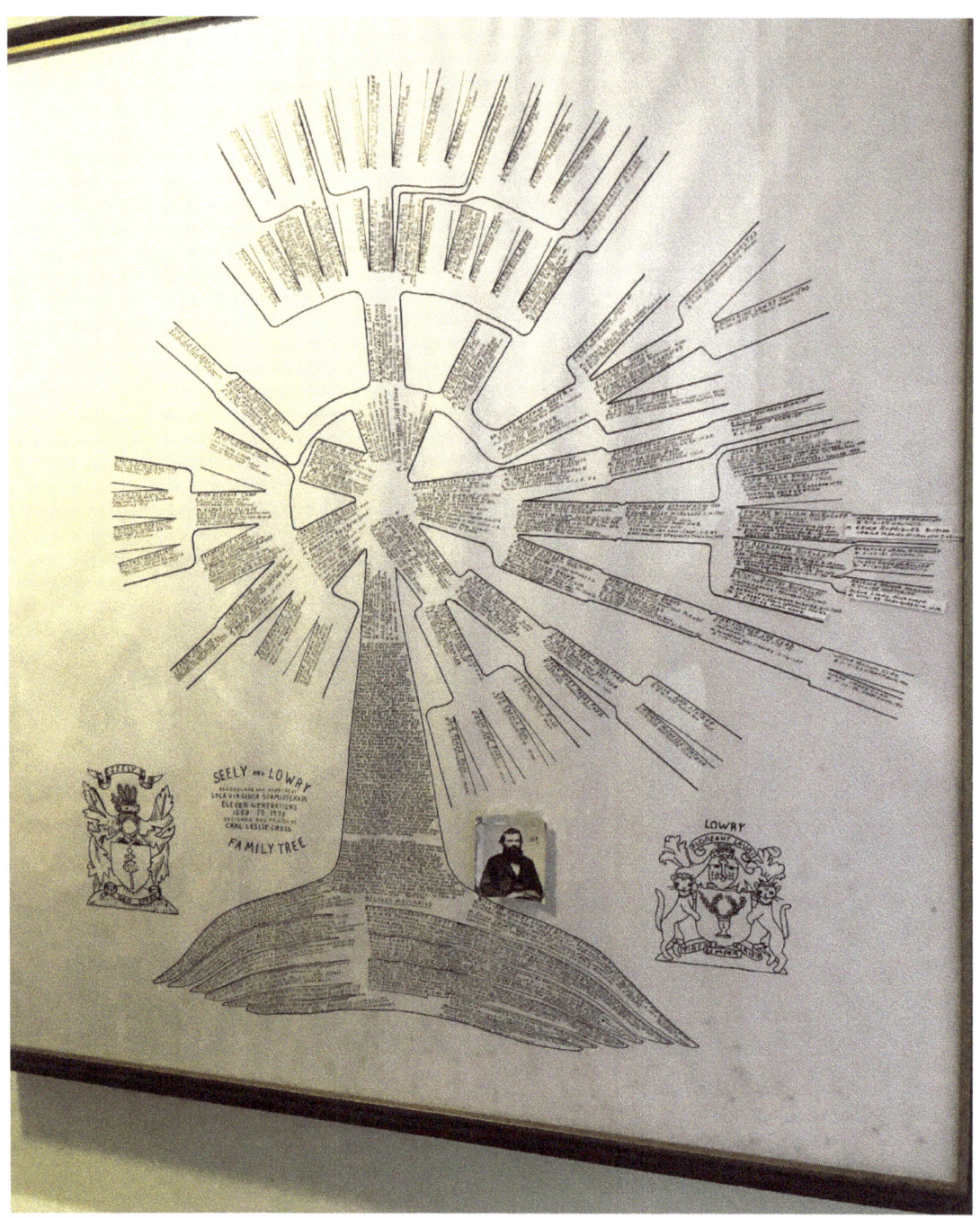

The little picture is my Great Grandfather, Clark Seeley, whose life is described on the trunk of the tree. On the right side are my five boys and their children.

For twenty years after Les retired, he and Mom traveled in a big motor home back and forth across this nation, traipsing through deserted cemeteries and court houses searching records. Mom included all the genealogy information she gathered into the book she printed in 1977: *A Grandmother's Life and Her Family History and Genealogy*.

One interesting thing to notice on these two trees is how many more children families had in the older times because so many died in childbirth and families needed children to help on the farms. There were nine children in my dad's family who lived on a farm in Wisconsin.

If a person can find that a member of his family came to this country on the Mayflower, the family line can be traced back to Charlemagne and the years 768-814. My mother discovered that our ancestor William Brewster came to this country on the Mayflower and so she sent for this chart from Scrooby Manor Press in Boulder, Colorado. (on the next page)

This makes me chain link Number 38 and my son Jim chain link Number 39.

Don't laugh! Check the chart with a magnifying glass. Well, you can laugh if you want to.

Since my mom did all this research before computers, her accomplishment is miraculous. I'm just glad I didn't have to do it!

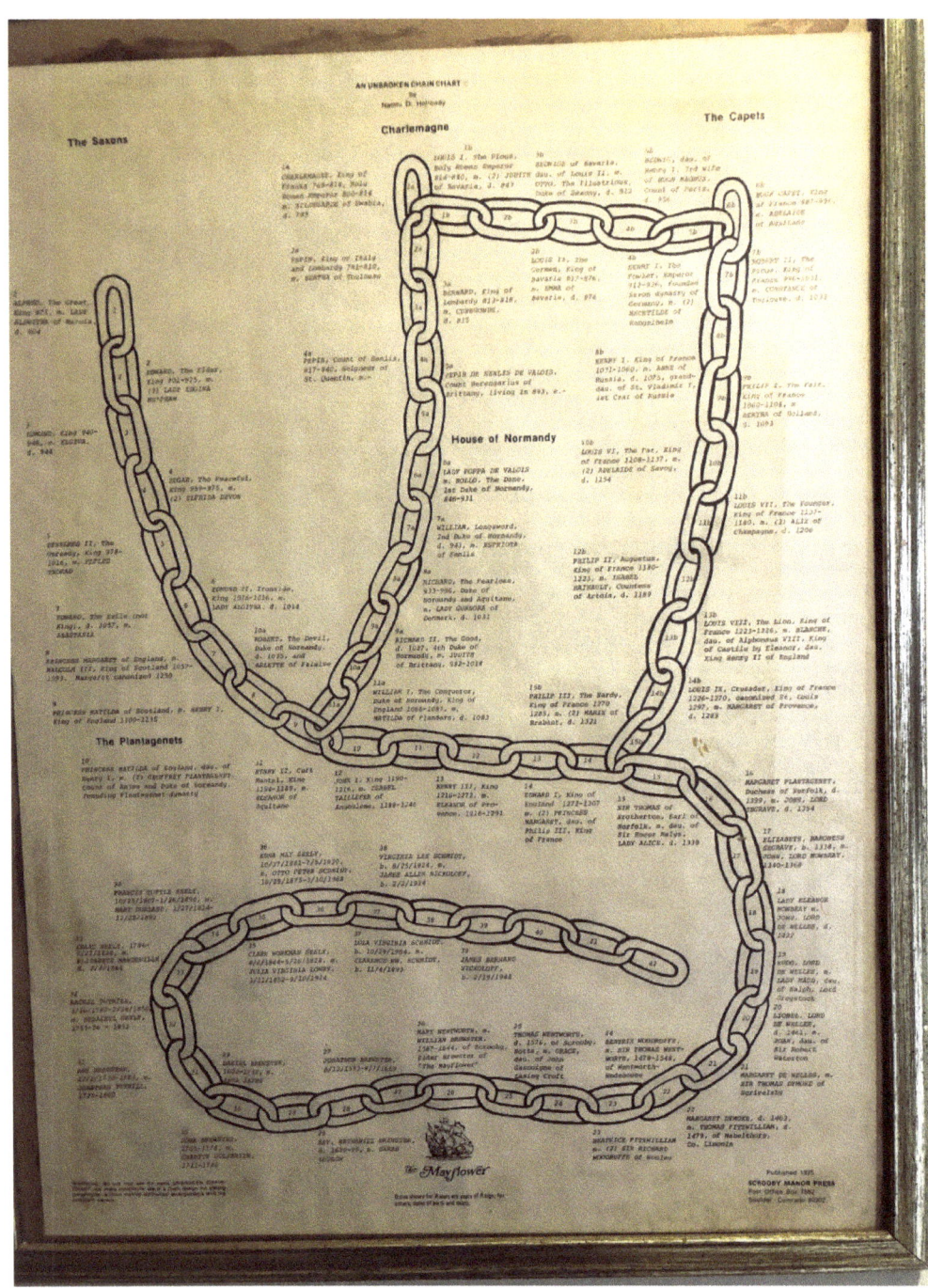

Chapter Twenty-Four
Photography

You have probably guessed by now that the camera is pretty much an extension of my right arm. I just can't resist grabbing the camera when I see something exciting or beautiful or fun or crazy. This chapter will just be pictures taken by a crazy old

lady.

This picture I took early in the morning before the shop was open on the walk to the River Ganges in India.

Son Jon's dinner production: crown roast of lamb

Jon creating gingerbread churches. His patience was amazing.

Elephant in Thailand painting the black pot for his flower picture I have hanging in my TV room.

Bob riding with zebras in Kenya.

Sheba and Mooney

On top of Table Mountain, I was watching men repelling with this view of Cape Town, South Africa.

Giraffe Manor, Nairobi, Kenya

Lewa Downs, Kenya

Riding an elephant in Nepal through this tall grass, the man in front of me dropped his film canister. His elephant's trunk searched and found it and picked it up and handed it to him. If I hadn't seen it with my own eyes, I wouldn't have believed it.

Paraty, Brazil, was a favorite port on our cruise from Buenos Aires to the Amazon. The church with the mountains behind it reminded me of Sierra Madre and our Passionist Fathers Monastery. When Americus Vespucci landed here, he is quoted as saying: "Oh God, if there were a paradise on earth, it wouldn't be far from here." I loved the colorful fishing boats.

Venice? Wrong. Las Vegas! I took this picture when I visited Jon not too long before he passed away

This picture I took of Victoria Falls from a helicopter in Zimbabwe. English explorers had heard about the falls but couldn't believe there was one as there were no mountains around. The Zambezi River, on the right, falls into a deep ravine causing the mist and then zig-zags into more ravines.

The red roofs at the head of the ravine are the Victoria Hotel where we stayed, so it was an easy walk to the falls. We did get soaked. Also saw some elephants on the way to and from. We were warned to watch their ears. If ears are lying flat, the elephant is happy. If the ears are flapping, avoid them. They were happy on the way to the falls, unhappy on the way back. On the road to the hotel there were signs saying, "Elephant crossing."

First, we saw big dung and then the culprits with ears flat. And then we were walking on the edge of the first gorge.

We finally got to the other end of the falls where the bridge spans the gorge connecting Zimbabwe with Zambia. It has a span of 650 feet. Taking pictures, I heard a bungie jumper yelling all the way down. I think he is the black speck near the bottom of this picture.

The best part of Zimbabwe was we got to ride an elephant and Bob took this picture of me with a baby. He was so sweet and gentle; his trunk around my neck.

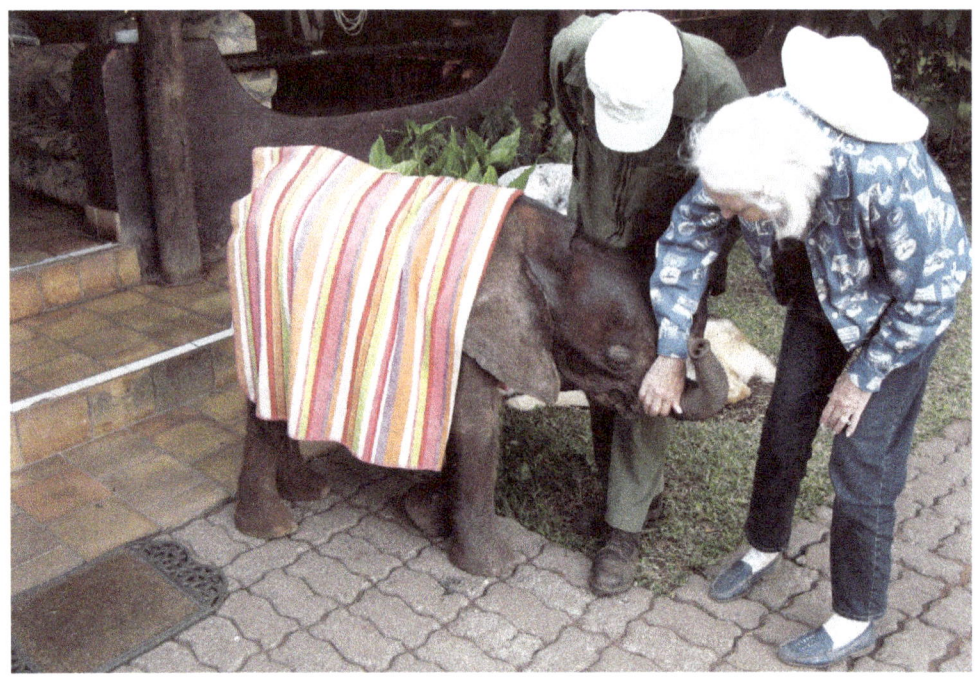

One of our favorite camps was Rekero Tented in Kenya. One morning they drove us to the edge of the Mara River and served us breakfast while we watched the hippos come down the opposite bank to take a bath and cool off.

    Campi Ya Kanzi was our first camp in Kenya. It was run by an Italian couple in conjunction with the Masai tribe. Our last night there, Antonella served cannelloni (my all-time favorite) followed by lamb chops, eggplant, zucchini with papaya for dessert. The whole Africa experience was so compelling I remembered a quote, "There are moments in life when you feel you are living 100%". I felt I was doing just that, and trying to express it, I really choked up. I hope that my readers may experience that feeling at least once in their lifetime.

I didn't realize I got this baby nursing while riding by on a bicycle rickshaw in India.

I took this big bad rhino with the long-distance lens (200 yards away).

Sierra Madre has built their own float every year to be in the Rose Parade. I took this picture at the parade when Bob and I went with the Fairfield Travel Club to California a few years ago. We watched them put the flowers on before the parade. Of course, I was ecstatic with the elephant theme.

Near Naples, Florida

This was hard to watch as these two lions tore a wart hog apart and devoured it. On the hill above was a hyena waiting to eat whatever they left.

Hyenas besides being the ugliest animal, they also make the most disgusting sound.

The only saving grace about the two previous pictures, is that a warthog is so ugly, and the lions had a good meal. Warthogs have a face and tusks only a mother could love as verified by my picture taken through the window at Giraffe Manor in Nairobi.

By contrast, I loved Mwangi's smiling face, our guide at Lewa Downs, Nairobi.

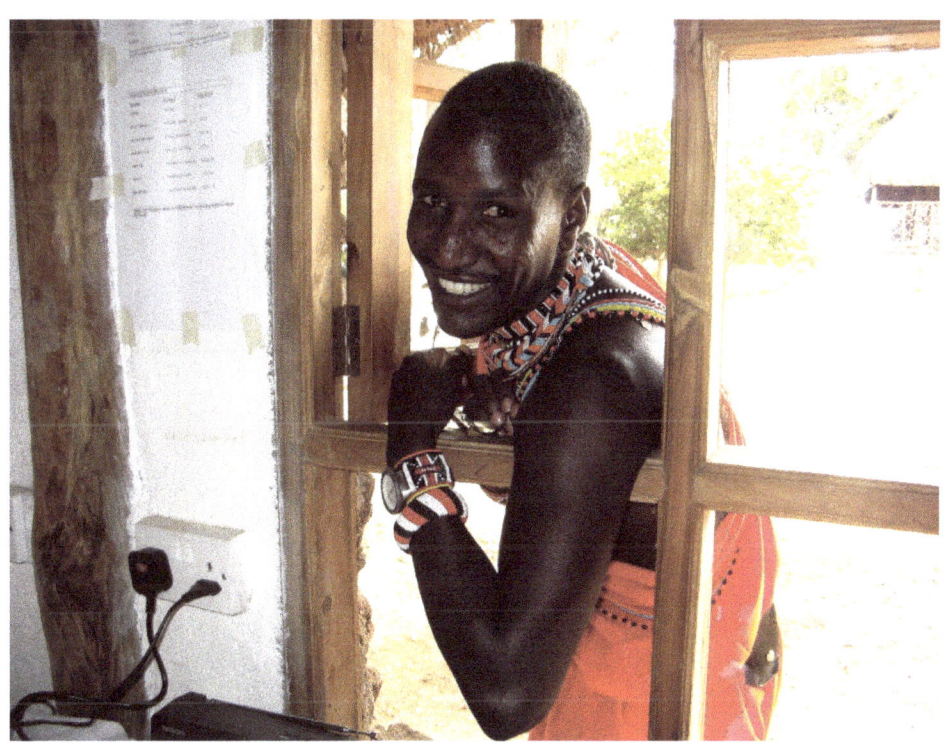

Bob on the ancient wall in Dubrovnik

Son Jim took this picture of me standing behind the headless statue in the Forum in Rome. It reminds me that I, too, was an ugly American. I had complained about U.S. sailors climbing all over the Acropolis. Deserved, a policeman bawled me out.

The owner put some kibble between his teeth and the giraffe took it out. I tried it.

I love the surprised look on Bob's face when the elephant took the hat off his mahout and put it on Bob's head.

One can't help loving giraffes. They are the antennas for the other animals and warn them of a hunting lion in the area and start running. They can kill a lion with their hoofs and are only susceptible to a lion attack when they are stretching their necks down for a drink of water. When they birth a baby, it drops six feet!

Chapter Twenty-Five

Memories

Seeing all these pictures again, the associated memories fly into my brain. The dictionary says memory is the accuracy and ease with which a person can retain and recall past experiences. For being in my Platinum Years, I surprise myself when my recollections are very clear with accompanying feelings. And then again, I can't remember what day it is!

I remember the happy positive feeling each time I threw a coin in the Trevi Fountain in Rome with the wish to come back and I did come back three more times.

The wonderful and yet nervous feeling as I stood on the edge of the island of Santorini overlooking the caldera. Who knows if the volcano might erupt again at that very moment? Scientists found ash from this eruption in Greenland.

When I see the picture below, I feel again that surprise and pleasure when Tony kissed me on my 56th birthday.

The heartbreak when I think of the last days I spent with my son Jon when Ken and he took me for a ride in the Red Rock Canyon and Las Vegas, Nevada.

This picture of my island in its fall dress, recalls the final resting place for the ashes of my husband, my Mom, and my son Tony. A strange thing happened when Jac paddled the canoe with Tony's ashes out to the island. Tom was on our dock and I was standing on my balcony watching Jac and a light airplane flew over and circled above. We all felt the same thing: it was my husband Jimmy flying over, paying his respects.

From pathos to the joyful surprise I felt when the next picture was taken. The Apple Valley Country Club was having a fashion show of clothes earlier than 1950. I had some wonderful 1920's flapper dresses that belonged to my Aunt Kathryn that were being modeled, and I modeled my wedding gown walking down the raised runway with Jimmy in his Navy uniform.

While he was waiting for his appearance, he was sitting at the club bar having a drink. Near Apple Valley was an air force base so some of the service men were also at the bar. Jimmy had left the Navy as an ensign with one gold stripe. One of the air force men said, "You are the oldest ensign I've ever seen."

A friend in the audience caught the moment (a passionate kiss in public).

The big laugh I had when I asked Bob to pull the arrow in the bow for a picture. It was so hard to pull that Bob couldn't budge it. These Masai men had a good laugh, too. Besides the bow and arrow, they had big knives to protect us from wild animals.

The pride I felt when Tony was presented with the Volunteer of the Year Award by the Mayor of Villa Rica for his volunteer service to the library. He taught a computer class to help people navigate the computer to get a job or for other needs.

The joy of finally experiencing the real Japan at the Minaguchiya Inn.

The pride a mother feels when her offspring performs a wondrous feat. Jim won much acclaim in the butterfly stroke. Jim started swimming competitively at eleven years old. From that time on he was up at 5 o'clock in the morning studying before leaving for swimming workout at 7 a.m. After school, he was again at the swimming pool. He had no time for baseball, football and soccer like his brothers. Butterfly was his special talent. He swam against Mark Spitz in the Nationals in Nebraska in 1966. Because of his academic record and swimming ability, U.S.C. granted him a 4-year scholarship. However, he chose a partial scholarship at Stanford.

PHS MERMEN—Chief hope from the Pasadena High School swim team at today's Foothill League championships at PHS is Jim Nickoloff. The former Marshall Junior High star, who set a CIF record while attending the Allen Ave., school, could win two events this afternoon.

At our recent family reunion in Hollywood, our family returned to Sierra Madre to walk again where the kids all grew up. We visited our little tract house and found the nickel and "off" the kids had pressed into the driveway cement so many years ago.

We visited the ball fields, the elementary school and Pasadena High School. Still exhibited in a trophy case was a big trophy Jim received as Athlete of the Year with his butterfly time still holding the record for the school. In his 70's, Jim is thinking about challenging the current Pasadena High School swim team to a race in the butterfly stroke.

The pride I felt, vicariously, when Jimmy caught this marlin in Mexico. It is hard to see but Jimmy put dark glasses on the eyes of the fish.

Even as a five-year-old, I remember how fun it was sitting on the floor by my Mom sewing and teaching me to read Dick and Jane. I also remember her breaking off a switch from the bush by the porch and how it hurt when she used it on my legs when I had been bad. Begging to go bare foot until Mom finally gave in, I went right out and took a little shovel to dig a hole and hit my big toe instead. Blood everywhere! My toenail did grow back.

It seemed that any time I did something my Mom didn't want me to do, I paid for it! I had a new one-piece pair of "beach pajamas" that had bell-bottom pants that I wanted to wear to school. Mom kept insisting they weren't appropriate, but I begged and begged and finally got my wish. At the first recess, I was running to get to the play equipment and tripped on the big pant leg, fell and broke my arm. See what I mean?

Chapter Twenty-Six
Prayer

My Platinum Years have quietly, but firmly brought prayer more consciously into my life. I was always a believer in the power of prayer but only said prayers to bless all my family and friends before I went to sleep. I do talk to every full moon addressing my departed sons and husband whom I know are living in Heaven. Everyone has some idea of what Heaven looks like. Jessie believes it is streets of gold.

I have a painting of Sherman Gardens, painted by my cousin Jean. It is a lovely place where Jean and I used to meet for lunch in Corona del Mar, California. Her painting on my wall depicts its beauty perfectly. I visualize Heaven looking like her painting.

Probably the first prayer I learned as an infant was: "Now I lay me down to sleep, I pray the Lord my soul to keep. And if I die before I wake, I pray the Lord my soul to take." This would be followed by my Dad saying "Nighty night, Snooks! Don't let the bedbugs bite!"

I have the perfect spot for sitting and watching the full moon rise over Lake Tara. It is a perfect spot to converse with God in his Heaven and thank him for all my blessings and I keep the cats happy by being "door lady". This morning's Bible reading from the Book of Micah (4:3) Nation shall not lift up sword against nation, neither shall they learn war anymore. My prayer: Let no one throw the first stone.

Son Tom was with me on the Fourth of July 2020, and we watched the full moon rise while the fireworks were going off from the dam. The moon had a bright reflection in the lake and the "rockets' red glare were bursting in air" and Tom and I burst out singing "were proof through the night, that our flag was still there! Oh say, does that star-spangled banner yet wave o'er the land of the free and the home of the brave." Certainly, a night I will never forget. I pray that this great country of ours will live on for many centuries to come and democracy will prevail over communism in China.

This picture was taken with Tom's cell phone from our dock on the Fourth of July.

When my son Tony and his wife Jessie moved in with me, I had a whole new understanding of Jesus and his love. They gave me a new Bible and three little books about Jesus to read each morning with my breakfast. I had read and studied the New Testament years ago, so I started reading two pages in the Old Testament each morning. The Old Testament is so full of war and destruction, I am happy to say that I have reached the New Testament and it is a pleasure to read about Jesus turning the other cheek.

Who could not believe in God when I see a sunrise over Lake Tara from my balcony?

When the Corona virus struck, Jessie copied the 91st Psalm and posted it by the front door and I added it to my daily breakfast time reading. If you have not read Psalm 91 recently, here is your chance to refresh your memory as Jessie posted it:

He who dwells in the secret place of the most High shall abide under the shadow of the Almighty.

I will say of the Lord, "He is my refuge and my fortress. My God; in Him I will trust

Surely, He shall deliver you from the snare of the fowler And from the perilous pestilence.

He shall cover you with His feathers and under His wings you shall take refuge His truth shall be your shield and buckler.

You shall not be afraid of terror by night; Nor of the arrow that flies by day.

Nor of the pestilence that walks in darkness; Nor of the destruction that lay waste at noonday.

A thousand may fall at your side. And ten thousand at your right hand; But it shall not come near you.

Only with your eyes shall you look and see the reward of the wicked.

Because you have made the Lord, Who is my refuge, Even the most High your dwelling place

No evil shall befall you. Nor shall any plague come near your dwelling place

For He shall give His angels charge over you to keep you in all your ways.

In their hands they shall bear you up Lest you dash your foot against a stone.

You shall tread upon the lion and the cobra. The young lion and the serpent you shall trample underfoot.

Because He has set His love upon me, therefore I will deliver Him. I will set Him on high, because He has known my name.

He shall call upon me and I will answer Him. I will be with Him in trouble. I will deliver Him and honor Him

With long life I will satisfy Him and show Him my salvation.

I loved the feeling of God giving me refuge under his wings so that I shall not be afraid of "the terror by night" nor the "pestilence that walks in darkness." "No evil shall befall you Nor shall any plague come near your dwelling For he shall give his angels charge over you..." Jessie is my personal angel.

Jessie flew to Jerusalem by herself and was enraptured by the whole experience, hoping to return, again, someday. She wants to see the Red Sea and Bethlehem on her next trip. She showed me a ram's horn called a Shofar she bought in Jerusalem and then tried to blow it. She blew and blew and suddenly, this blast came out and scared both of us and our cat Sheba half to death!

This picture I took of Rafael's angel in a church in Copenhagen gives me the feeling of the power of angels to protect us under their wings.

Jessie also prepares a page of Bible sayings for me to read each morning:

--Let my flesh/body be restored and become fresher than in youth;
Let me return to the days of my youthful strength (Job 33:25)

--Those who wait on the Lord
Shall renew their (my) strength
I shall mount up with wings like eagles
I shall walk and not grow tired (Isaiah 40:31)

--Even in old age, I will still bear fruits and prosper and thrive
I will stay fresh and green. (Psalms 92:14)

--The Lord fills my life with good things.
My youth is renewed like the soaring eagle (Psalms 103:5)

--The Lord is the strength of my life (Psalms 27:1)

--God gives me a spirit of love and a sound mind (Timothy 1:7)

I love the feeling this prayer gives me and I really feel like flying like eagles and staying "fresh and green" after I read it.

In addition to the above morning reading, I also read two pages in *An Introductory Dictionary of Theology and Religious Studies*, a 1515-page tome edited by my son Jim and Orlando O. Espin, a professor at the University of San Diego. There are over 60 contributors covering definitions of words used in all religions including the beliefs of Christians, Jews, Buddhists, Muslims, the American Indians and the Aztecs. Over the years, I met some of the contributors to this dictionary.

I told Jim only a mother would read such a dictionary. But it is fun to come across a definition written by my son. Currently, I have reached the M's and have learned about Thomas More (1478-1535), the Book of Mormon, Mitzvah, Moses and, on page 915, the meaning of Mudra as explained by Todd T. Lewis.

I met Todd in Kathmandu in 1999. That was the trip where I met son Jim in New Delhi, India. We took a plane from there to Nepal. Todd was on a sabbatical from Holy Cross doing research on Buddhism. He took us on a tour of the main Buddhist temples including Swayambhunath Stupa, its nickname Monkey Temple. On this day, the crowd, with red dots on their foreheads, were lined up on the street as a parade went by. On a float was a statue of Avolakateshvara, sometimes identified as the "son" of the Buddha Amitabha. I was so excited to see "her, him, it," also known as Kwan Yin in China, riding on a float in a parade.

Years ago, I was a docent at the USC Pacific Asia Museum in Pasadena, California. Every three months, the museum changed its displays to show articles from the places Captain Cook visited in the Pacific Rim during his sailing days. To prepare us for each exhibit, the museum had experts explain the subject matter. A woman lecturer from U.C.L.A. spoke about Avolakateshvara and she just rolled that name off her tongue! I went home and practiced saying it until I, too, could roll it off my tongue! And so, I surprised Jim and Todd when I pronounced it with authority!

When we were landscaping the house in Apple Valley after the Oriental remodel, I found a statue of Avolakateshvara at a nursery. They loaded her up in the trunk of my car. When I got home, I told Jimmy and his golfing friend that I had a body in the trunk of my car. It was Avolakateshvara whom I renamed: Madam Su Ling.

Jac and his wife Debra with Madam Su Ling in Georgia. On the left you can see a little bit of the Japanese lantern.

The power of God's strong hand is felt when we experience earthquakes, wildfires, hurricanes, tornados and flood. In my 96 years, I have experienced all of the above except a tornado. For me, the most frightening was earthquakes. The magnitude of the strength of the Lord when the earth moves under you is unbelievable. By contrast, with the exception of lightning, most wildfires are caused by human carelessness. But the Lord's hand does create the wind that causes the massive spreading of the fires. He also controls the rain that could put them out.

Earthquakes terrify me! Perhaps because of the first one I experienced when I was only nine years old. It was a 6.4 in Long Beach, California. I was in grade school at the time, but the nearby junior high school was putting on a performance of "Little Women" after school. I walked the few blocks to Jefferson Junior High School and then walked home after the play.

It was almost 6 o'clock and Mom was stirring something on the stove while I told her about the play. All of a sudden, there was this big roar and Mom thought it was an airplane crashing nearby. I was paralyzed as dishes and canned goods came flying out of the cupboards. She grabbed me and as we went between the table and the wall, our built-in ice box came out of the wall onto the table in front of us and blocked our way. With the next movement, the ice box went back in the wall and Mom pulled me out to the four porch steps. The quake then knocked us down the steps face first into the driveway and broke my Mom's wristwatch. She took me out to the front yard grass and told me she was going through the neighborhood to turn off the gas lines. My mom, always practical! Terrified, I was on hands and knees hanging onto the grass as the earth kept shaking. Actually, the earth kept shaking off and on for over six months. That memory will never leave me. My fear never lessened with subsequent quakes over the years.

It was March 10, 1933, a 6.4 quake and a date I will never forget. It changed the whole building code as all the brick buildings tumbled down and the roof of the school auditorium I had just left fell on the seats. If the quake was a few minutes earlier, I wouldn't be writing this!

Wildfires were a worry in Sierra Madre as the dry mountain above the town was always in danger of someone's carelessness. We had a volunteer fire department and they always managed to get the fires out before they reached our town. Unfortunately, with fires all up and down the west coast, the fires are uncontrolled as I write this. This morning news broadcast said that a 39-year-old firefighter lost his life in the Bobcat fire above Sierra Madre. I do pray every day for the wind to stop and the rain to come to put out the fires in California and Colorado.

Since living in Georgia, I have experienced a few hurricanes, one that caused the lake to rise half-way up the back yard. I had always wished that my house was closer to the lake. Be careful what you wish for. God is still very much in charge!

One of my favorite prayers Jessie wrote out for me is attributed to Rabbi Yechiel Eckstein:

Even in Old Age

Do not cast me away when I am old;
Do not forsake me when my strength is gone.

Psalm 71:9

According to Jewish tradition, Psalm 71 was composed by David during the rebellion led against him by his son Absalom. In David's younger days, when he was often pursued by King Saul, David was sustained by the promise that he would one day ascend to the throne and live out his life. This time, however, David was already 65. His youth was behind him, and old age was before him. He worried that this battle could be his last and this would be the end of his life. In this psalm David cried out to God, "Do not cast me away when I am old; do not forsake me when my strength is gone."

The Jewish sages elaborate on the conversation that David held with God during this perilous time. According to the sages, David said to God, "When I was young and strong, I put my life in danger to lead Your sons, the children of Israel, into battle. But now that I have grown old, they no longer appreciate me and they say, "When will he die, and his name perish? (Psalm 41:5). God responded with words from the prophet Isaiah, "Even to your old age and gray hairs I am he. I am he who will sustain you. I have made you and I will carry you; I will sustain you and I will rescue you" (Isaiah 46:4). And indeed, God did just that. David was victorious and returned to Jerusalem as the King of Israel.

David's passionate words in this psalm, asking God to be with him in his old age, have become particularly meaningful to all who are fortunate enough to make it to their "golden years." It is a blessing to live a long life, but it's not merely existence that we aspire toward: we want life with meaningful relationships and experiences, the ability to contribute, and the peace of having our needs met. Too frequently, old age is a time of vulnerability and a source of fear for so many. This verse and this psalm serve as a healing balm that reassures us that God will be with us even in our final years. We need not fear for He will be with us.

The sages teach that this verse can also apply to times in our life when we are young. There are times when we feel tired, weary, and are lacking vitality. Just as the old can still be young at heart, there are young people who are old at heart. For those times as well, this psalm is a potent prayer.

Let's take comfort in David's words and God's promise in Isaiah. God is with us on our first day and our last –and every day in between.

I especially love the last line. You may be wondering why Jessie would give me a prayer written by a Jewish rabbi. Jessie has been looking for a church to join for a long time. She seems to prefer the Pentecostal Church's spontaneous verbal responses and singing, but she occasionally attends the synagogue where Rabbi Eckstein presides because it is a Jewish synagogue that believes in Jesus Christ. Located in Marietta, it is a long drive for Jessie.

Sometimes I attend a local church with Jessie, but often she works on Sundays. More often I spend Sundays with my son Tom. We share our praise and thankfulness to God, and then watch the Braves or the Falcons on TV.

I may be starting my Titanium Years, but I don't expect to live as long as Methuselah who lived 969 years. My wish for anyone who reads this book is to enjoy each and every minute, day and year of your life and take the following prayer seriously:

PRAYER FOR THE AGED

Lord, Thou knowest better than I know myself that I
    am growing older and will someday be old.

Keep me from getting talkative, and particularly from
    the fatal habit of thinking I must say something
    on every occasion.

Release me from craving to try to straighten out every-
    body's affairs.

Keep my mind free from the recital of endless details—
    give me wings to get to the point.

I ask for grace enough to listen to the tales of others' pains.
Help me to endure them with patience.

But seal my lips on my own aches and pains—they are
increasing and my love of rehearsing them is
becoming sweeter as the years go by.

Teach me the glorious lesson that occasionally it is possible
that I might be mistaken.

Keep me reasonably sweet, I do not want to be a saint—
Some of them are hard to live with, but a sour old
person is one of the crowning works of the devil.

Make me thoughtful, but not moody; helpful but not bossy.
With my vast store of wisdom, it seems a pity not
to use it all—but Thou knowest, Lord, I want a few
friends at

The end.

www.ingramcontent.com/pod-product-compliance
Lightning Source LLC
Chambersburg PA
CBHW040419130526
44592CB00052B/2851